Series/Number 07-095

# BOOTSTRAPPING
# A Nonparametric Approach
# to Statistical Inference

**CHRISTOPHER Z. MOONEY**
*West Virginia University* and
*University of Essex*

**ROBERT D. DUVAL**
*West Virginia University*

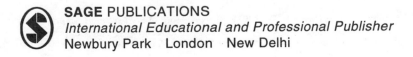

**SAGE** PUBLICATIONS
*International Educational and Professional Publisher*
Newbury Park   London   New Delhi

*For information address*:

SAGE Publications, Inc.
2455 Teller Road
Newbury Park, California 91320

SAGE Publications Ltd.
6 Bonhill Street
London EC2A 4PU
United Kingdom

SAGE Publications India Pvt. Ltd.
M-32 Market
Greater Kailash I
New Delhi 110 048 India

Printed in the United States of America

Library of Congress Catalog Card No. 89-043409

Mooney, Christopher Z.
    Bootstrapping: a nonparametric approach to statistical inference /
Christopher Z. Mooney, Robert Duval.
        p.    cm.—(Quantitative applications in the social sciences; 95)
    Includes bibliographical references.
    ISBN 0-8039-5381-X
    1. Social sciences—Statistical methods.   2. Bootstrap
(Statistics)   3. Inference.   I. Duval, Robert.   II. Title.
III. Series: Sage university papers series. Quantitative
applications in the social sciences; no. 95
HA 31.2.M66   1993
300'.1'5195—dc20                                                                93-5212

93  94  95  96  10  9  8  7  6  5  4  3  2  1

Sage Production Editor:  Susan McElroy

---

When citing a university paper, please use the proper form. Remember to cite the current Sage University Paper series title and include the paper number. One of the following formats can be adapted (depending on the style manual used):

(1) MOONEY, CHRISTOPHER Z., and DUVAL, ROBERT D. (1993) Bootstrapping: A Nonparametric Approach to Statistical Inference. Sage University Paper series on Quantitative Applications in the Social Sciences, 07-095. Newbury Park, CA: Sage.

*OR*

(2) Mooney, C. Z., & Duval, R. D. (1993). *Bootstrapping: A nonparametric approach to statistical inference* (Sage University Paper series on Quantitative Applications in the Social Sciences, series no. 07-095). Newbury Park, CA: Sage.

# CONTENTS

# SERIES EDITOR'S INTRODUCTION

In social science research, there is a long-standing interest in nonparametric statistics, which do not rely on such weighty assumptions as normality. Many of the established univariate and bivariate "distribution-free" statistics are reported in our excellent series monographs *Nonparametric Statistics: An Introduction* (no. 90) and *Nonparametric Measures of Association* (no. 91), by Dr. Jean Dickinson Gibbons. This current monograph by Professors Mooney and Duval takes yet another step away from the classical parametric approach to inference. Bootstrapping uses the computer to "resample" an original sample extensively, inductively arriving at an estimate of a statistic's sampling distribution. (Following the authors, one might use Monte Carlo methods to draw 1,000 random samples *with replacement* of size 50 from an original sample of 50, each time calculating, say, $\hat{\beta}$. The frequency distribution of these 1,000 $\hat{\beta}$'s would form the estimate of the sampling distribution.) Then this estimated sampling distribution (rather than an a priori assumed distribution) is used to make population inferences, such as that beta's value is different from zero.

Hence bootstrapping can apply when the underlying sampling distribution of the statistic cannot be assumed normal, as when estimating a regression coefficient with ordinary least squares in the presence of skewed residuals. Also, bootstrapping may serve when the sampling distribution has no analytic solution, such as the difference of two sample medians. In such situations, rather than a classical approach to confidence intervals (and significance testing), one may favor four bootstrap confidence interval methods: normal approximation, percentile, bias-corrected percentile, or percentile-*t*. Although each method has distinct advantages and disadvantages, as Mooney and Duval carefully discuss, they give a slight nod to the percentile-*t* method, at least if hypothesis test accuracy is the chief goal. Moreover, even if the analyst ultimately relies on classical inference methods, he or she can employ bootstrapping to assess the violation of certain model assumptions.

To illustrate bootstrapping, the authors offer numerous real data examples, from oil production in the American states, per capita personal income in SMSAs, ratings of members of Congress by Americans for Democratic Action, and median preference differences between legislative committee members and the whole legislature. Finally, in the Appendix, the authors provide a convenient summary of how to apply this computer-intensive methodology using various available software packages. The analyst, armed with this monograph and appropriate computer support, should be able to explore readily the inferential opportunities bootstrapping affords.

—*Michael S. Lewis-Beck*
Series Editor

## ACKNOWLEDGMENTS

Sections of this monograph were first presented at the Eighth Political Methodology Conference at Durham, North Carolina, in July 1991. We would like to acknowledge the helpful comments of the participants of that conference, especially John Freeman, Philip A. Schrodt, Gary King, Doug Rivers, and Mel Hinnich. We are also indebted to the following for their input on this project: George Krause, Bradley Efron, Robert Stine, Keith Krehbiel, Thomas J. DiCiccio, William Jacoby, Michael Lewis-Beck, and two anonymous reviewers.

# BOOTSTRAPPING
# A Nonparametric Approach
# to Statistical Inference

**CHRISTOPHER Z. MOONEY**
*West Virginia University* and
*University of Essex*
**ROBERT D. DUVAL**
*West Virginia University*

## 1. INTRODUCTION

A fundamental task of quantitative social science research is to make probability-based inferences about a population characteristic, $\theta$, based on an estimator, $\hat{\theta}$, using a sample drawn from that population. Bootstrapping is a computationally intensive, nonparametric technique for making such inferences. Bootstrapping differs from the traditional parametric approach to inference in that it employs large numbers of repetitive computations to estimate the shape of a statistic's sampling distribution, rather than strong distributional assumptions and analytic formulas. This allows the researcher to make inferences in cases where such analytic solutions are unavailable, and where such assumptions are untenable. The bootstrap is not, therefore, a statistic per se. Rather, it is an approach to using statistics to make inferences about population parameters. But it is fundamentally different from the traditional parametric approach of the $z$ and $t$ test in which social scientists have been schooled for the past 70 years.

Bootstrapping relies on an analogy between the sample and the population from which the sample was drawn. The central idea is that it may sometimes be better to draw conclusions about the characteristics of a population strictly from the sample at hand, rather than by making perhaps unrealistic assumptions about that population. Bootstrapping involves "resampling" the data with replacement many, many times in order to generate an empirical estimate of the entire sampling distribution of a statistic. The use of subsampling in statistical inference is not new (e.g., Jones, 1956; McCarthy, 1969; Tukey, 1958), but what is new

1

2

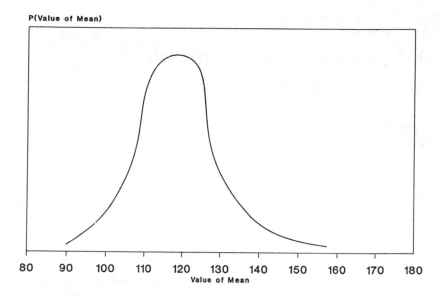

P(Value of Mean)

| | | | | | | | | | | |
|---|---|---|---|---|---|---|---|---|---|---|
| 80 | 90 | 100 | 110 | 120 | 130 | 140 | 150 | 160 | 170 | 180 |

Value of Mean

Figure 1.1. Sampling Distribution of the Mean IQ for a Hypothetical Introductory Sociology Class ($n = 10$)

and interesting about the bootstrap is the expansion of this idea in a very general way to a wide variety of statistics, through the use of cheap and abundant computer power.

In order to understand what bootstrapping is and how it differs from traditional parametric statistical inference, one must first be clear about the concept of the sampling distribution. The sampling distribution of a statistic, $\hat{\theta}$, can be thought of as the relative frequency of all possible values of $\hat{\theta}$ calculated from a sample of size $n$ drawn from a given population (Mohr, 1990, pp. 13-28). Given random sampling from the population, $\hat{\theta}$ is a random variable, with a sampling distribution that is a function of $\theta$. For example, consider the mean IQ of a sample of 10 students from an introductory sociology class of 300 students (the population). The sampling distribution of this sample mean would consist of the probability of getting each possible value of mean IQ from this class. This probability would likely be low for the values of 90 or 150, and higher for a value of 120. Also, it might be slightly skewed to the right, as it would be likely that more students with extremely high

IQs would be enrolled than those with extremely low IQs. We could construct a sampling distribution empirically by drawing an infinitely large number of 10-student samples from this class, and creating a frequency distribution of their mean IQ scores. Figure 1.1 displays one such possible distribution.

Intuitively, it seems likely that the shape and location of this sampling distribution would be influenced by such things as the overall mean of IQs in the class ($\theta$), the dispersion of these IQs, and the size of the sample. And of course graduates of even the most introductory of statistics courses know that this is indeed the case. However, what is equally important is that the relationship between these factors can vary across different statistics. For instance, the shape of the sampling distribution of the sample mean is not necessarily the same as that of the sample median, even for the same sample size and population.

An appreciation of the factors that can influence the shape of $\hat{\theta}$'s sampling distribution is important, because it is our estimate of this sampling distribution that allows us to make inferences to $\theta$ from $\hat{\theta}$. We typically make these inferences in one of two ways. First, we test hypotheses about $\theta$ in terms of the probability of getting the value of $\hat{\theta}$ we have gotten, given what we think $\hat{\theta}$'s sampling distribution is. Alternatively, we might use this sampling distribution to develop intervals around $\hat{\theta}$ in which we are reasonably sure that $\theta$ will be found. In both of these cases, the sampling distribution is at the center of statistical inference.

Both bootstrap and parametric inference have the same underlying purpose: Using limited information, estimate the sampling distribution of a statistic, $\hat{\theta}$, to make inferences about a population parameter, $\theta$. The key difference between these inferential approaches is how they obtain this sampling distribution. Whereas traditional parametric inference uses a priori assumptions about the shape of $\hat{\theta}$'s distribution, bootstrapping estimates the entire sampling distribution of $\hat{\theta}$ by relying on the analogy between the sample and the population. For instance, in the case of the sample mean, bootstrapping will use the sample data as if they were the population and empirically build a picture of the sampling distribution of the sample mean. Traditional parametric inference relies on the central limit theorem, which states that the sample mean has a normal distribution under certain conditions. Although this is actually a trivial case, owing to the power of parametric inference in most instances with the sample mean, it will be used extensively throughout this monograph because of its familiarity. Bootstrapping has its greatest practical importance when we turn to statistics and situations for which the sampling distribution is either unknown or intractable—for example, the difference between two sample medians or an ordinary least squares (OLS) regression coefficient where the residuals are nonnormal.

## Traditional Parametric Statistical Inference

In practical statistical situations, we rarely know for certain the shape or location of $\hat{\theta}$'s sampling distribution. After all, if we had this kind of information, we would have little need to draw inferences from a limited sample. Rather, to make inferences from a sample to a population, we must estimate this sampling distribution. The traditional parametric approach to this task is (a) to assume that $\hat{\theta}$'s sampling distribution has a shape with known probability properties (e.g., a normal distribution), and (b) to estimate analytically the parameters of that sampling distribution (e.g., the mean and standard deviation of a normal distribution) (Maritz, 1981, p. 1; Tiku, Tan, & Balakrishnan, 1986, p. iii).

For many commonly used statistics, such as the sample mean and OLS regression coefficients, these steps to estimating the sampling distribution are often routine. For example, there are good theoretical reasons to believe that the sample mean is distributed normally under certain conditions that may frequently be met. Consider the distribution of the average height of random samples of 10 women. If we assume that women's height is normally distributed in the population (as is likely), the sampling distribution of the average height of samples of women will also be normal (Mansfield, 1986, p. 237). Based on this assumption and deduction, our estimate of the mean of this distribution is the mean of the sample, $\overline{X} = \Sigma x_i/n$. Our estimate of the standard deviation of the sampling distribution is the sample standard deviation of the mean, $\hat{\sigma}_{\overline{X}} = \hat{\sigma}/\sqrt{n}$, where $\hat{\sigma}$ is the sample estimate of the standard deviation of the underlying variable. So if we draw a random sample of 10 women whose average height is 5'9'' with a standard deviation of 3'', our estimate of the sampling distribution of the sample mean of women's heights (for $n = 10$) would be that it (a) is normally distributed, (b) is centered on 5'9'', and (c) has a standard deviation of .95'' (i.e., $3/\sqrt{10}$).

Once we have deduced $\hat{\theta}$'s sampling distribution using this parametric assumption and the analytic formulas associated with it, we can use it to make inferences about $\theta$. This can be done by hypothesizing a location for $\theta$ (and for $\hat{\theta}$'s sampling distribution, given $\theta$'s hypothesized

P(Estimator Value)

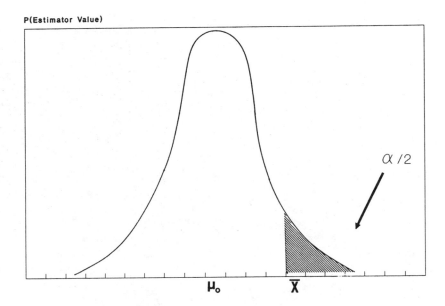

Figure 1.2. Null Hypothesis Assuming a Normal Distribution

location), and testing this hypothesis against the sample statistic, using the tabled probabilities of the assumed distribution.

Suppose we are interested in whether or not the mean ($\mu$) height of women in the U.S. population equals 5'6''. We set up our null hypothesis (the rejection or acceptance of which will answer our research question) so that the population mean equals 5'6''. Because the sample mean is an unbiased indicator of the population mean, this null hypothesis also implies that the sampling distribution of the sample mean is centered at $\mu_0$ (5'6''), and is normally distributed with a standard deviation of $\hat{\sigma}/\sqrt{n}$ (.95''). This null hypothesis can be pictured as in Figure 1.2.

To test this hypothesis, we calculate $\overline{X}$ from the sample data and see whether it falls "too far" (in terms of standard errors) from this hypothesized $\mu$ for us to believe that the null hypothesis is true, given the probability of $\overline{X}$ taking on that value under this hypothetical distribution. We do this by standardizing the difference between the hypothesized value of $\mu$ and the calculated value of $\overline{X}$. The estimated standard deviation of $\overline{X}$ and the Student's $t$ table are then used to derive the

P(Estimator Value)

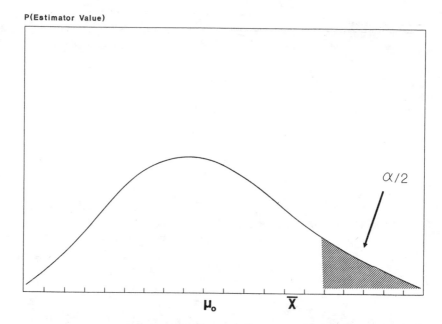

Figure 1.3. "True" Sampling Distribution

probability that we would have come up with such a value for $\overline{X}$ if our hypothesized value for $\mu$ held true in the population. In our example, if $\mu_o = 5'6''$, $\overline{X} = 5'9''$, $\hat{\sigma}_{\overline{X}} = .95''$, and $n = 10$, then:

$$t_{observed} = (5'9'' - 5'6'')/.95 = 3.16.$$

As the probability of observing a $t$ score of 3.16 with 9 degrees of freedom is less than .025, we might well reject the null, and infer that the average height of women in the United States is not 5'6''.

Two aspects of this familiar exercise are especially relevant to the discussion of the bootstrap. First, this parametric $t$ test is a test of a hypothesis ($\mu = \mu_o$) that is based on an assumption about $\overline{X}$'s sampling distribution [$(\overline{X} - \mu_o)/\hat{\sigma}_{\overline{X}} \sim t_{df = n-1}$]. If *either* of these conditions is not met, an inferential error could be made. For example, suppose we assume a sampling distribution for $\overline{X}$ as in Figure 1.2, but in fact $\overline{X}$ is distributed as in Figure 1.3. This could occur if women's height was not normally distributed in the population, as we have a small sample. At the given $\alpha$ level, our assumption of normality would lead us to reject the null, whereas if we knew the true distribution, we might well not reject it.

Because substantively we are concerned only with the hypothesis, $\mu = \mu_0$, the chance that the parametric assumption, $(\overline{X} - \mu_0)/\hat{\sigma}_{\overline{X}} \sim t_{df = n - 1}$, is invalid increases the possibility of incorrectly evaluating the null regarding the population mean. That is, we may conclude that $\mu \neq \mu_0$ either because $\mu \neq \mu_0$ or because the sample mean is not distributed as a $t$. If the statistic of interest is not distributed as assumed, the parametric test of inference is invalid. That is, we cannot make accurate probability statements about our null, because we do not know the probability $(\alpha)$ of rejecting a true null (Type I error) or the probability $(\beta)$ of failing to reject a false one (Type II error).

Consider the annual oil production of U.S. states, a variable that is highly skewed owing to truncation at zero and a few states (such as Texas and Alaska) with high values. If a researcher wanted to make statements about the average annual state production from a sample of 20 states, the parametric approach of assuming normality for $\overline{X}$ would be inappropriate. Figure 1.4 displays a Monte Carlo estimate of the sampling distribution of the average oil production for 1985, where $n = 20$. This distribution clearly does not appear normal, and the Kolmogrov-Smirnov (K-S) test confirms this observation.[1] Assuming normality in this case could well lead to an erroneous probability statement regarding a hypothesis test on the population mean. Such a situation could occur with the small sample mean of any bounded aggregate variable, such as per capita income, number of conflicts per year, or the size of a state's congressional delegation.

It is only in rare cases that parametric assumptions allow for an exact estimation of the sampling distribution of $\hat{\theta}$ (DiCiccio & Romano, 1989; Efron, 1987). Typically, the parametric approach gives only a more or less close approximation of this distribution. This is by no means a categorical condemnation of the parametric approach, as these approximations are often very good. The important point here is that other types of approximations may well be as good as or better than the parametric approximation in certain situations.

The second aspect of the discussion of parametric inference that is relevant to the bootstrap is that parametric inference also requires estimates of the parameters of the assumed sampling distribution, such as the standard deviation and mean in the case of a normal distribution.

8

P(Value of Mean)

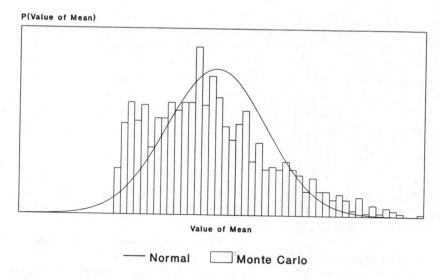

Value of Mean

——— Normal   ⬜ Monte Carlo

Figure 1.4. Monte Carlo Estimate of the Sampling Distribution of 1985 Mean
State Oil Production ($n = 20$; trials = 5,000)
SOURCE: Data from Dye and Taintor (1991).
NOTE: Both distributions have the same mean and standard deviation.

That is, not only do we need to be able to assume that $\hat{\theta}$'s sampling
distribution has known probability properties, we also need tractable
point estimators of the parameters of that distribution. Although the
sample mean has well-known analytic formulas for estimating these
quantities, some statistics (such as the difference between two sample
medians) have no such formulas, thereby precluding the use of parametric inference (Efron & Tibshirani, 1986, p. 55).[2]

Traditional parametric inference requires, then, both a distributional
assumption about $\hat{\theta}$ and a readily available method for calculating the
parameters of that distribution. When either of these requirements is not
met, there is the potential for serious problems in practical statistical
inference. For example, a researcher might apply an inappropriate
distributional assumption to the statistic of interest and risk worsening
the $\alpha$ and/or $\beta$ error rates. Although we routinely set $\alpha$ to some level at
which we are comfortable risking a Type I error, the violation of
distributional assumptions means that our true $\alpha$ level may well differ
from what we select under the assumption of normality.

The requirements of parametric inference can raise another kind of problem if they force the researcher to use a less-than-ideal statistic to measure a characteristic simply because that statistic has a known sampling distribution. The problem here is bias in the measure of the phenomenon. For example, suppose a researcher is interested in the difference between the median preference of two groups, such as a congressional committee and its parent chamber (Hall & Grofman, 1990; Krehbiel, 1990). The ideal estimator in this situation is the difference between two sample medians, but the properties of the sampling distribution of this statistic are not known.[3] The researcher might instead use the difference between two sample means, because the shape of its distribution is known under certain conditions. The problem is that any inferences made about the difference of population medians from the difference of sample means may well be tenuous. (See Chapter 3 for an extension of this discussion.)

The traditional parametric approach to inference is therefore some- times less than ideal. Except in those few happy situations where the characteristic of interest is best measured by a statistic with a sampling distribution of known properties and tractable parameter formulas, the researcher using traditional inferential statistics must settle for a greater than nominal error rate.

## Bootstrap Statistical Inference

The bootstrap allows the researcher to make inferences without mak- ing these strong distributional assumptions[4] and without the need for analytic formulas for the sampling distribution's parameters, thereby avoiding the dilemma outlined above. Instead of imposing a shape on $\hat{\theta}$'s sampling distribution by assumption, bootstrapping involves empiri- cally estimating the *entire sampling distribution* of $\hat{\theta}$ by examining the variation of the statistic within the sample. To be sure, the bootstrap retains the same model structure; for example, a bootstrapped linear regression is still a linear regression. With bootstrapping, it is simply the inferential foundation that is different.

The basic bootstrap approach is to treat the sample as if it is the population, and apply Monte Carlo sampling to generate an empirical estimate of the statistic's sampling distribution. Recall that the sampling distribution of $\hat{\theta}$ can be thought of as the distribution of the values of that statistic calculated from an infinite number of random samples of size $n$ from a given population. Monte Carlo sampling takes this conception literally, building an estimate of the sampling distribution by drawing a large number of samples of size $n$ randomly from a population, and calculating the statistic for each of these samples. This random sampling is an empirical simulation of the random component of the statistic being estimated. The relative frequency distribution of these $\hat\theta$ values is an estimate of the sampling distribution for that statistic.

True Monte Carlo estimation requires full knowledge of the population, but of course this is not usually available in practical research settings. Typically, we have only a sample drawn from this population, which is why we need to infer $\theta$ from $\hat\theta$ in the first place.

In bootstrapping, we treat the sample as the population and conduct a Monte Carlo-style procedure on the sample. This is done by drawing a large number of "resamples" of size $n$ from this original sample randomly *with replacement*. So, although each resample will have the same number of elements as the original sample, through replacement resampling each resample could have some of the original data points represented in it more than once, and some not represented at all. Therefore, each of these resamples will likely be slightly and randomly different from the original sample. And because the elements in these resamples vary slightly, a statistic, $\hat\theta^*$, calculated from one of these resamples will likely take on a slightly different value from each of the other $\hat\theta^*$'s and from the original $\hat\theta$. *The central assertion of bootstrapping is that a relative frequency distribution of these $\hat\theta^*$'s calculated from the resamples is an estimate of the sampling distribution of $\hat\theta$.*

The steps of the generic bootstrapping procedure can be stated more formally (Efron, 1979, pp. 2-3; Efron & Tibshirani, 1986, pp. 54-55; Hinckley, 1988, pp. 322-324). Consider the one-sample case, where a simple random sample of size $n$ is drawn from an unspecified probability distribution, $F$, so that $X_i \sim _{ind}F$. In the general case, the $X$ is the random component of the model being tested (e.g., the variable in the case of a sample mean model, or the error term in a regression model), and $x$ is the sample realization of $X$. The basic steps in the bootstrap procedure are as follows:

1. Construct an empirical probability distribution, $\hat F(x)$, from the sample by placing a probability of $1/n$ at each point, $x_1, x_2, \ldots, x_n$. This is the empirical distribution function (EDF) of $x$, which is the nonparametric maximum likelihood estimate (MLE) of the population distribution function, $F(X)$ (Rohatgi, 1984, pp. 234-236).[5]

2. From the EDF, $\hat{F}(x)$, draw a simple random sample of size $n$ with replacement. This is a "resample," $x_b^*$.

3. Calculate the statistic of interest, $\hat{\theta}$, from this resample, yielding $\hat{\theta}_b^*$ .

4. Repeat steps 2 and 3 $B$ times, where $B$ is a large number. The practical magnitude of $B$ depends on the tests to be run on the data. Typically, $B$ should be 50-200 to estimate the standard error of $\hat{\theta}$, and at least 1,000 to estimate confidence intervals around $\hat{\theta}$ (Efron & Tibshirani, 1986, sec. 9).

5. Construct a probability distribution from the $B$ $\hat{\theta}_b^*$'s by placing a probability of $1/B$ at each point, $\hat{\theta}_1^*$ , $\hat{\theta}_2^*$ , . . . , $\hat{\theta}_B^*$ .[6] This distribution is the *bootstrapped estimate of the sampling distribution of* $\hat{\theta}$, $\hat{F}^*(\hat{\theta}^*)$. As will be discussed in Chapter 2, this distribution can be used to make inferences about $\theta$.

The justification for this procedure rests on the analogies of the sample EDF with the population distribution function that generated the data and the random resampling mechanism with the random component of that process. The EDF is the nonparametric MLE of the unknown distribution $F(X)$ (Rao, 1987, pp. 162-166; Rohatgi, 1984, pp. 234-236). That is, given that we have no other information about the population, the sample is our single best estimate of that population.[7] We therefore treat the sample as the population and use Monte Carlo sampling to generate a series of resamples from the original sample. These resamples are analogous to a series of independent random samples from $F(X)$. The sampling distribution of a statistic, $\hat{\theta}$, can be estimated by calculating that statistic for each of these resamples. This Monte Carlo procedure can be done directly on the population when the population is known (Noreen, 1989, chap. 3), but when only a sample is available, we rely upon the fact that this sample is the nonparametric MLE of the population.

A simple example may serve to clarify this procedure. Although the sample mean, $\overline{X}$, may be evaluated quite easily in most cases without the bootstrap,[8] it provides a good example because of its familiarity. Consider the data in Table 1.1, where the second column contains 30 cases generated randomly from a standard normal population. This is the original sample. The third through sixth columns contain four resamples from these data. The bottom rows display the mean and standard deviation of each column.

Notice that each resample is somewhat different from the original sample. There are no values in any of the resamples that do not appear in the original sample, but in a given resample some of the original

12

TABLE 1.1
Example of Bootstrap Resampling

| Case Number | Original Sample[a] | Resample 1 | Resample 2 | Resample 3 | Resample 4 |
|---|---|---|---|---|---|
| 1 | 0.697 | −0.270 | −1.768 | −0.270 | −0.152 |
| 2 | −1.395 | 0.697 | −0.152 | −0.152 | −1.583 |
| 3 | 1.408 | −1.768 | −0.270 | −1.779 | −0.787 |
| 4 | 0.875 | 0.697 | −0.133 | 2.204 | −0.101 |
| 5 | −2.039 | −0.133 | −1.395 | 0.875 | −0.914 |
| 6 | −0.727 | 0.587 | 0.587 | −0.914 | 0.697 |
| 7 | −0.366 | −0.016 | −1.234 | −1.779 | −0.727 |
| 8 | 2.204 | 0.179 | −0.152 | −2.039 | −0.727 |
| 9 | 0.179 | 0.714 | −1.395 | 2.204 | −0.787 |
| 10 | 0.261 | 0.714 | 1.099 | −0.366 | −1.779 |
| 11 | 1.099 | −0.097 | −1.121 | 0.875 | −0.787 |
| 12 | −0.787 | −2.039 | −0.787 | −0.457 | −1.121 |
| 13 | −0.097 | −1.768 | −0.016 | −1.121 | −1.583 |
| 14 | −1.779 | −0.101 | 0.739 | −0.016 | −0.914 |
| 15 | −0.152 | 1.099 | −1.395 | −0.270 | −1.234 |
| 16 | −1.768 | −0.727 | −1.415 | −0.914 | −1.395 |
| 17 | −0.956 | −1.121 | −0.097 | −0.860 | 2.204 |
| 18 | 0.587 | −0.097 | −0.101 | −0.914 | −1.779 |
| 19 | −0.270 | 2.204 | −1.779 | −0.457 | −0.366 |
| 20 | −0.101 | 0.875 | −1.121 | 0.697 | 0.875 |
| 21 | −1.415 | −0.016 | −0.101 | 0.179 | 2.204 |
| 22 | −0.860 | −0.727 | −0.914 | −0.366 | 2.204 |
| 23 | −1.234 | 1.408 | −2.039 | 0.875 | −0.101 |
| 24 | −0.457 | 2.204 | −0.366 | −1.395 | −1.121 |
| 25 | −0.133 | −1.779 | 2.204 | −1.234 | 2.204 |
| 26 | −1.583 | −1.415 | −0.016 | −1.121 | −0.097 |
| 27 | −0.914 | −0.860 | −0.457 | 1.408 | −0.914 |
| 28 | −1.121 | −0.860 | 2.204 | 0.261 | −0.101 |
| 29 | 0.739 | −1.121 | −0.133 | −1.583 | −1.779 |
| 30 | 0.714 | −0.101 | 0.697 | −2.039 | 0.714 |
| Mean | −0.282 | −0.121 | −0.361 | −0.349 | −0.325 |
| St. dev. | 1.039 | 1.120 | 1.062 | 1.147 | 1.234 |

a. Characteristics of the generating population for the original sample: $X \sim N(0,1)$.

values are represented more than once, and some not at all. In Resample 1, for example, the value $x = -1.395$ (Case 2 in the original sample) is not found. On the other hand, the value $x = -0.860$ (Case 22 in the original sample) is found twice. Each resample is made up of members

P(Value of Mean)

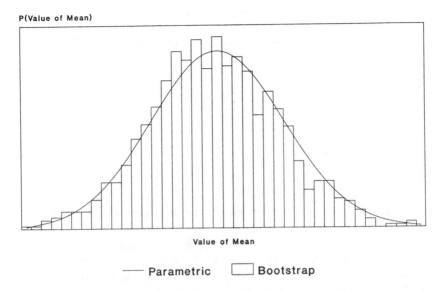

Value of Mean

—— Parametric    ☐ Bootstrap

Figure 1.5. Bootstrap Versus Parametric Sampling Distribution of the Sample Mean of a Normally Distributed Variable ($n = 30$)

SOURCE: Data from Table 1.1.

of the set of the original sample, but it does not comprise an identical set. As a consequence, the mean and standard deviation of each resample vary from those of one another and from those of the original sample, although they are similar.

A total of 1,000 resamples were drawn from the original data, and the mean was calculated for each resample. The frequency distribution of these 1,000 resample means, $\overline{X}_b^*$, is the bootstrapped estimate of the sampling distribution of the mean of this variable for a sample size of 30. The appearance of the normality of this bootstrapped distribution in Figure 1.5 is confirmed by a K-S test.[9] This is an indication that this bootstrapped sampling distribution is a good estimate of the underlying sampling distribution of $\overline{X}$, because we have good theoretical reasons to believe that this statistic is normally distributed in this circumstance, as discussed above.

Comparing the specific characteristics of this bootstrapped sampling distribution with that of the known theoretical distribution of this sample mean provides further evidence of the accuracy of $\hat{F}^*(\hat{\theta}^*)$ in this

TABLE 1.2
Characteristics of Parametric and Bootstrapped Sampling Distributions for the Mean of the Simulated Data in Table 1.1

| *Method of Estimation* | $E(\overline{X})$ | $\hat{\sigma}_{\overline{X}}$ | *2.5th Percentile* | *97.5th Percentile* |
|---|---|---|---|---|
| Parametric | −.282 | .1897 | −.6538[a] | .0898[a] |
| Bootstrap | −.282 | .1911 | −.6544[b] | .0910[b] |

NOTE: $N = 30$; $B = 1{,}000$.
a. Calculated as $\overline{X} \pm z_{.025}\hat{\sigma}_{\overline{X}}$.
b. Taken directly from the histogram of $\overline{X}^*_b$ displayed in Figure 1.5.

case. Table 1.2 displays some summary statistics of this $\hat{F}^*(\overline{X}^*)$ and the distribution derived analytically from the assumed normal sampling distribution of $\overline{X}$. As can be seen, both the expected values and the estimates of the standard deviations of these distributions are almost identical. The 2.5th and 97.5th percentiles of each are also quite similar. On a variety of criteria, then, this bootstrapped sampling distribution appears to be a very good estimate of what we know to be the true sampling distribution of this statistic.

Figure 1.6 displays an example of the bootstrapped sampling distribution of the mean of 1985 growth in gross U.S. state product, for a sample of 20 states. This figure parallels Figure 1.5, in that it shows the $\hat{F}^*(\overline{X}^*)$ for a small sample mean of a normally distributed variable. As with the simulated-data example in Figure 1.5, the bootstrapped sampling distribution here closely approximates what we would expect theoretically.

Of course, all this extra effort is unnecessary for these sample means because the traditional parametric approach provides a good estimate of $\hat{F}(\hat{\theta})$, with efficient and adequate inferential tests. However, these examples are useful both to demonstrate the generic bootstrap procedure and to provide an early evaluation of the bootstrap's performance. Because we have strong theoretical and empirical evidence about the characteristics of the sampling distribution of the sample mean, it is a good first test of the bootstrap. And as Table 1.2 and Figures 1.5 and 1.6 indicate, the bootstrap has performed well here. However, the practical usefulness of the bootstrap will be shown only if it performs well in cases where traditional parametric inference is inapplicable. We will examine several such situations in Chapter 3.

P(Value of Mean)

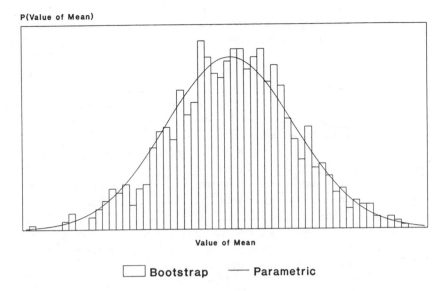

Value of Mean

☐ Bootstrap ——— Parametric

Figure 1.6. Bootstrap Versus Parametric Sampling Distribution of the 1985 Mean Growth in Gross State Product ($n = 20$)

SOURCE: Data from Dye and Taintor (1991).

## Bootstrapping a Regression Model

As with all statistics, traditional parametric inference regarding co-efficients in a regression model is based upon distributional conditions and assumptions that may or may not hold true for a given set of data. For example, the Gauss-Markov theorem holds that OLS estimators will be normally distributed if the model's error is normally distributed, and the central limit theorem assures us that this error will be normal if the sample size is "large." However, if these conditions do not hold in a particular model and data set, parametric inferential statements about OLS estimators may be inaccurate. It is in cases such as this that bootstrapping may be useful (see Chapter 3).

The regression model provides a useful example of the bootstrapping procedure in that as a multiparameter model, its random component is made obvious, and not embedded in a measured variable, as in the case of the sample mean. This is important because it is this random component of a model that must be resampled in bootstrapping, and this is made clear in bootstrapping a regression model.

Consider a standard linear regression model:

$$Y = X\beta + \epsilon, \tag{1}$$

where $X$ is an $(n \times k)$ matrix of exogenous variables, $\beta$ is a $(k \times 1)$ vector of regression coefficients, and $Y$ is an $(n \times 1)$ vector of response variables. $\epsilon$ is an $(n \times 1)$ vector of error terms, that is, the random fluctuation of $Y_i$ around $\hat{Y}_i$, the predicted value of $Y$ for a given set of values for the exogenous variables.

This regression model can be bootstrapped in two ways. At issue is which quantities are to be resampled. The most straightforward method is simply to resample entire cases of data; that is, resample rows in the data matrix. $B$ resamples of size $n$ would be generated in this way, and the regression model estimated for each resample. This would result in a $(B \times k)$ matrix of bootstrapped regression coefficients, each column of which would contain $B$ $\hat{\beta}_k^*$'s. These $\hat{\beta}_k^*$'s can be converted into an estimate of the sampling distribution of $\hat{\beta}_k$ in the usual way, by placing a probability of $1/B$ at each value of $\hat{\beta}_k^*$.

The problem with this approach is that it ignores the error structure of the regression model (Freedman, 1981, 1984). Recall that the whole point of resampling is to mimic the random component of the process. With a single sample statistic, such as the sample mean, this random component is embedded in the measured variable. But in regression analysis, the process is more complex. The classic regression model holds that the regressors are fixed constants, and that the response is a function of these fixed constants and a random error term (Draper & Smith, 1981, p. 7). The only random aspect of the process is the error term, $\epsilon_i$, and therefore it is this quantity that should be resampled in bootstrapping.

Bootstrapping an estimated regression coefficient by resampling the observed errors, or residuals, is somewhat more complicated than resampling cases, however (Freedman, 1981; Hall, 1988a, p. 37). First, we draw a simple random sample of cases from the population, and measure the exogenous and response variables for these cases. Next, we estimate $\beta$ using, for example, the OLS method. Using this estimate, $\hat{\beta}$, and the values of the observed variables, we calculate the residuals:

$$\hat{\epsilon}_i = Y_i - \hat{Y}_i, \tag{2}$$

where $\hat{Y} = X\hat{\beta}$. A resample of these residuals is then drawn randomly with replacement. Next, we generate a bootstrapped vector of the response variable for this resample, by adding the resampled vector of residuals to the vector of fitted response values from the sample:

$$Y_b^* = \hat{Y} + \hat{\epsilon}_b^*. \tag{3}$$

These bootstrapped responses, $Y_b^*$, are then regressed casewise on the (fixed) exogenous variables to estimate a bootstrapped vector of estimated coefficients, $\hat{\beta}_b^*$, for this resample:

$$Y_b^* = X\hat{\beta}_b^* + \hat{\epsilon}. \tag{4}$$

This procedure, from residual resample to the estimation of $\hat{\beta}_b^*$, is repeated $B$ times. The bootstrapped regression coefficients for each resample are placed in a row in a $(B \times k)$ matrix. Each column in this matrix of bootstrapped regression coefficients can then be converted into an estimate of the sampling distribution of $\hat{\beta}_k$, by placing probability of $1/B$ on each value of $\hat{\beta}_b^*$ for a given parameter $\beta_k$, as described above.

In choosing between the resampling cases and residuals approaches, a researcher needs to consider the stochastic component of the model. In the general case, it is theoretically most justifiable to resample this portion of the model. Therefore, most theoretical statisticians suggest the resampling of residuals (Freedman, 1981, 1984; Hall, 1988a, p. 37; Shao, 1988). But whereas in true experiments the regressors can be fixed (indicating that residuals should be resampled), most social scientists do not work with experimental data (Stine, 1990, p. 255). In most survey research, for example, regressor values are as random as the responses. Because of this, resampling cases in much social scientific analysis may be most appropriate. The question should be evaluated for any individual study based on the stochastic component of the model and data under consideration.

Just as was done for the sample mean above, consider examples of bootstrapping a bivariate regression model where all the traditional parametric assumptions hold, using both simulated and real-world data. The parametric sampling distribution is a good estimate of the true sampling distribution in this case, and as such provides another assessment of the bootstrap's performance. Table 1.3 displays the characteristics of the sampling distributions estimated by the parametric and

TABLE 1.3

Characteristics of Parametric and Bootstrapped Sampling
Distributions for a Simple OLS Regression Coefficient With All
Assumptions Justified (simulated data)

| Method of Estimation | $E(\hat{\beta})$ | $\hat{\sigma}_{\hat{\beta}}$ | 2.5th Percentile | 97.5th Percentile |
|---|---|---|---|---|
| Parametric | 1.986 | .180 | 1.617[a] | 2.355[a] |
| Bootstrap | 1.985 | .177 | 1.637[b] | 2.332[b] |

NOTE: $N = 30$; $B = 1,000$. Population characteristics: $\beta = 2.0$; $\sigma_\epsilon = .25$, fixed independent variable values. Residuals resampling.
a. Calculated as $\hat{\beta} \pm t_{df = 29;.025}\hat{\sigma}_{\hat{\beta}}$.
b. Taken directly from the corresponding histogram of $\hat{\beta}_b^*$'s displayed in Figure 1.7.

residuals resampling approaches using simulated data, and Figure 1.7
displays these distributions graphically. The residuals resampling approach was used here because the data were generated with fixed values
for the independent variable. The bootstrapped sampling distribution

P(Value of Est. Coefficient)

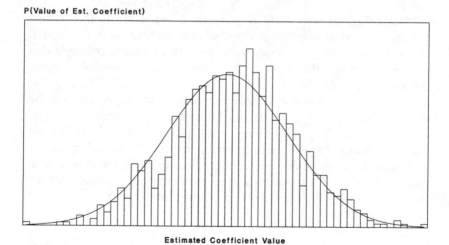

Estimated Coefficient Value

☐ Bootstrap ——— Parametric

Figure 1.7. Estimated Sampling Distributions for OLS Regression Slope With
Normal Error Using Simulated Data ($n = 30$)
NOTE: Residuals resampling.

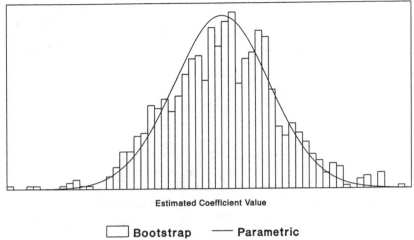

Estimated Coefficient Value

☐ Bootstrap    —— Parametric

Figure 1.8. Sampling Distributions of the OLS Slope of Per Capita Personal Income on Percentage of High School Graduates

SOURCE: Data from U.S. Census (1979).
NOTE: Cases resampling.

for this regression coefficient clearly provides a close approximation to the parametric distribution, just as for the mean of a normal variable discussed above. The expected value, the standard deviation, and the key percentile points are quite similar to one another. And because we have good theoretical reasons to believe that the parametric estimate is an accurate representation of the true sampling distribution in this circumstance, we can say that the bootstrap estimate closely approximates the true sampling distribution here.

Figure 1.8 displays the parametric and bootstrap sampling distribution for the coefficient resulting from regressing per capita personal income in 141 standard metropolitan statistical areas on the percentage of high school graduates in 1979 (U.S. Bureau of the Census, 1979). The cases resampling approach was used here because the independent variable was not fixed. In these data, the errors are approximately normally distributed and meet the other OLS assumptions. As with the bootstrapped sampling distribution of the mean, this real-data example parallels the simulated-data example with which it is paired (with a

20

slight overestimate of dispersion), indicating further the accuracy of the $\hat{F}^*(\hat{\theta}^*)$ in this situation. Although the stochastic component of the bootstrapping process causes the bootstrap histograms displayed in Figures 1.7 and 1.8 to be somewhat irregular, in both of these cases the bootstrapped sampling distributions pass the K-S test for normality.

**Theoretical Justification**

At this point, it is important to discuss *why* bootstrapping works as well as it does in the above examples. At root is the idea that if the sample is a good approximation of the population, bootstrapping will provide a good approximation of the sampling distribution of $\hat{\theta}$ (Efron & Stein, 1981). The theoretical arguments developed here are not technical. Examples of the extensive technical literature on this subject include work by Singh (1981), Bickel and Freedman (1981), Freedman (1981), and Efron (1987). The purpose of this section is to give the reader a sense of the basic arguments justifying the bootstrap.

The conceptual justification of the bootstrap procedure rests on the analogies of (a) the sample EDF with the population distribution function (PDF) that generated the data, and (b) the random resampling mechanism with the stochastic component of the model. The theoretical justification for these analogies is based on two levels of asymptotics.

First, as the original sample size ($n$) approaches the population size ($N$), the EDF [$\hat{F}(x)$] approaches the true distribution [$F(X)$] (Bickel & Freedman, 1981; Singh, 1981). This makes intuitive sense, in that as a sample increases in size, it contains more and more information about the population, until $n = N$, $\hat{F}(x) \approx F(X)$.[10] This notion is transparent in the analytic standard error formula for most statistics' standard errors, in that they are inversely proportional to sample size. For example, $\hat{\sigma}_{\bar{x}} = \hat{\sigma}/\sqrt{n}$.

The second level of asymptotics involved in proving the consistency of the bootstrap has to do with how accurately the bootstrapped sampling distribution, $\hat{F}^*(\hat{\theta}^*)$, approximates $F(\hat{\theta})$ in a given sample when $n$ is large enough to allow $\hat{F}(x)$ to approach $F(X)$. Under this condition, as the number of resamples, $B$, increases to infinity, Babu and Singh (1983) show that $\hat{F}^*(\hat{\theta}^*) \approx F(\hat{\theta})$. Again, this is similar to the definitional conception of the sampling distribution employed in Monte Carlo sampling from the population (Noreen, 1989, chap. 3). Under simple random sampling with replacement, the resamples will vary randomly from the original sample, and the $\hat{\theta}^*$'s calculated from these resamples will likewise vary randomly from the original $\hat{\theta}$. Put another way, as a random variable generated as a function of $\hat{\theta}$, $\hat{\theta}^*$ is distributed randomly in the same way as $\hat{\theta}$. Resampling mimics this random process, and as we get more and more resamples, the process is more and more closely approximated.

Therefore, the theoretical justification for the bootstrap rests on the assertions that (a) as the original sample size increases to infinity, the EDF approaches the PDF, and (b) if the original sample size ($n$) is large enough, as the number of resamples ($B$) increases to infinity, $\hat{F}^*(\hat{\theta}^*)$ approaches the sampling distribution of the original estimator.

Although mathematical proof of consistency is important justification for any proposed statistical procedure, for the researcher using that procedure the criterion of practicality also needs to be considered. How large an $n$ and $B$ are "large enough" to provide satisfactory results? This is an empirical question that depends on the statistics to be estimated and the accuracy desired (Efron, 1979, sec. 2). The size of $B$ is merely a computational concern because, with a looping algorithm, it is strictly a function of program running time. However, the improvement of $\hat{F}^*(\hat{\theta}^*)$ as an estimator of $F(\hat{\theta})$ is slight for $B > 1,000$, in most cases (Efron & Tibshirani, 1986, sec. 9).

Sample size is more problematic, however, because it is a function of a project's experimental design. Some experimenters have had difficulty with the accuracy of the bootstrap for samples on the order of 10-20 (Schenker, 1985), and others have expressed confidence in bootstrap results even with these very small samples (e.g., Bickel & Krieger, 1989; Efron, 1982, chap. 5; Stine, 1985). Few, however, dispute the quality of the approximation of $F(X)$ with $\hat{F}(x)$ when $n$ reaches the range of 30-50, and when the sampling procedure is truly random. The bootstrap is therefore practical within the limits of most empirical social science analysis.

Two problems can arise here, however. The most obvious one is that if the EDF is not a good approximation of the PDF, the bootstrapped estimate of the sampling distribution of $\hat{\theta}$ will be inaccurate. This lack of congruence between the PDF and the EDF could arise because of a small sample, a biased sample design, or merely random bad luck. One can account for this by making the sample design as sound as possible, in terms of sample size, stratification, and so forth. Once a sample has been chosen, however, little can be done nonparametrically to improve the fit between the EDF and the PDF. Of course, if one has some prior information about the population or the sample, parametric inference techniques can be used to mitigate a bad sample. For example, if one knew from prior experience or theory that

$\hat{\theta}$'s sampling distribution was normal, this information could be included in the analysis. But if one does not have any such information, the single best estimate we have about the PDF is the EDF. Bootstrapping is then the best general way to take full advantage of all the information about the population that is contained in the sample.

The second problem that can arise from using the EDF as an estimate of the PDF is that whereas the latter is a continuous function for a continuous variable, the EDF is always a discrete function. That is, although there are infinite numbers of values a continuous variable can take on, the number of values a sample takes on is always finite. For example, the 30 values drawn randomly from a standard normal distribution displayed in the second column of Table 1.1 could be constructed into an EDF, but as we move from one value to the next highest, there is always a "jump," or a set of values of the variable that are not represented in the EDF that are represented in the PDF. So whereas the PDF is a smooth function, the EDF has a stair-step appearance. As the sample size increases, the "steps" in the EDF get closer and closer together, and the function gets smoother and smoother, but it remains discrete. Figure 1.9 compares the cumulative EDFs of samples of size 10 and 60 drawn randomly from a normally distributed variable, showing how the steps smooth out as sample size increases.

The effect of this phenomenon on bootstrapping in practice is that in between the steps of the EDF are values of the PDF that cannot be included in the analysis. If those values included and left out of the EDF are evenly and randomly distributed, this should not affect the accuracy of the results. But if this is not the case (e.g., with a small or biased sample), the accuracy of the bootstrap could suffer. It is in such cases that having prior knowledge (i.e., being able to make parametric assumptions) about the variables and estimators is very helpful. There is also some discussion in the bootstrapping literature that the application of "smoothing" processes to the EDF would help fill in the gaps in a useful way (Silverman & Young, 1987). Semiparametric inference of this nature is in its early stages of development, however, and the extent of its practical advantages remains to be seen.

## The Jackknife

The jackknife is an inferential technique that is closely related to the bootstrap. Developed in the late 1940s and 1950s, the jackknife has been

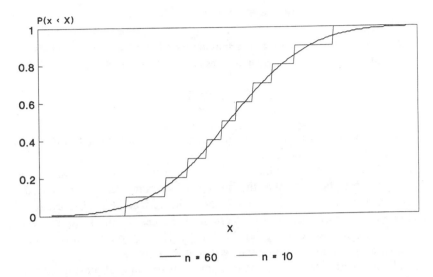

Figure 1.9. Cumulative Distribution Functions of a Random Normal Variable With Different Sample Sizes

used both to estimate and compensate for bias in statistical estimates and to derive robust confidence intervals. Like the bootstrap, the jack-knife assesses the variability of a statistic by examining the variation within the sample data, rather than through the use of parametric assumptions. The jackknife is a less general technique than the boot-strap, however, and it explores a sample's variation in a different way. The jackknife's primary uses today are likely to be in making inferences in cases of complex sampling, and for identifying outlying data points.

If the bootstrap's motto is "Sample with replacement," the jackknife's motto is "Drop one out." That is, jackknifed statistics are developed by systematically dropping out subsets of the data one at a time and assessing the variation in the $\hat{\theta}$ that results (Miller, 1974, p. 1; Quenouille, 1949, 1956).[11] The steps in jackknifing $\theta$ are as follows:

1. Divide the sample into $g$ exhaustive and mutually exclusive subsamples of size $h$, such that $gh = n$.
2. Drop out one subsample from the entire original sample. Calculate $\hat{\theta}_{-1}$ from that reduced sample of size $(g-1)h = n - h$.
3. Calculate the "pseudovalue," $\tilde{\theta}_g$, from this $\hat{\theta}_{-1}$ by weighting as follows:

$$\tilde{\theta}_g = g\hat{\theta} - (g-1)\hat{\theta}_{-1}. \tag{5}$$

4. Repeat steps 2 and 3 for all $g$ subsamples, yielding a vector of $g$ $\tilde{\theta}_g$'s.

5. Take the mean of these pseudovalues to yield the jackknifed estimate of $\theta$, $\tilde{\theta}$:

$$\tilde{\theta} = g^{-1} \sum \tilde{\theta}_g. \tag{6}$$

A key consideration in jackknifing is the size, $h$, of the $g$ subsamples. In his original development of the technique, Quenouille (1949) used only two subsamples, splitting his sample in half. But he soon generalized the choice of $h$ to be 1, so that the number of subsamples would equal the number of elements in the sample (1956). This reduced the arbitrariness of the assignment of $h$ and $g$, and is probably the best form of the jackknife to use in most situations (Miller, 1974, p. 2). The exception to this is in the case of a complex sampling plan, as discussed below.

The most common use of the jackknife has been in estimating the bias of $\hat{\theta}$. $\tilde{\theta}$ is second-order unbiased, and a simple estimate of the first-order bias of $\hat{\theta}$ can be developed by subtraction:

$$\text{Estimate}[\text{BIAS}(\hat{\theta})] = \tilde{\theta} - \hat{\theta}. \tag{7}$$

This technique has been used to estimate and reduce bias in estimators known to be biased, such as the ratio of two sample means (Mantel, 1967; Rao & Beegle, 1967).

Tukey (1958) moved beyond simple bias estimation to develop a method of using the jackknife to test hypotheses regarding $\theta$. He suggested that the $g$ pseudovalues could be considered to be approximately independent and identically distributed random variables in many situations, particularly when $\hat{\theta}$ has a locally linear quality (Miller, 1974, p. 8). He used this property to develop a robust "jackknifed $t$ statistic" to be used in conducting hypothesis tests:

$$t_{\text{jack}} = \frac{g^{1/2}(\tilde{\theta} - \theta_0)}{[(g-1)^{-1} \sum (\tilde{\theta}_g - \tilde{\theta})^2]^{1/2}}, \tag{8}$$

where $\theta_0$ = the value of $\theta$ in the null hypothesis. This test statistic has been shown to be distributed as the Student's $t$ with $g - 1$ degrees of freedom, as either $g$ or $h$ goes to infinity, for many widely used statistics, such as the mean, the product-moment correlation coefficient, the Wilcoxon signed-rank statistic, and linear regression coefficients (Miller, 1974, p. 6; see also Brillinger, 1964; Miller, 1964).

To clarify the jackknife's development, consider the example of jackknifing a sample mean. The second column of Table 1.4 contains the same 30 cases of randomly generated values from a standard normal variable that were used in the initial bootstrapping example in Table 1.1. We jackknife the mean of these values using each case as a subset, so that $g = 30$ and $h = 1$. The third column displays the $\hat{\theta}_{-1}$ for each case, that is, the value of $\hat{\theta}$ calculated after dropping that case out. The fourth column displays the weighted pseudovalues for each case, $\theta_g$. Notice that in this example, the pseudovalues are quite close to the values of the original data. Further note that the jackknifed estimate of $\theta$, $\hat{\theta}$, is quite close to the original estimate, $\hat{\theta}$. This is what we would expect, considering that we are working with an unbiased estimator of the population parameter. Just as with the bootstrap example using these data (Table 1.2), the fact that the jackknife has given these confirmatory results is a suggestion of its accuracy. The difference between the parametric and jackknife $t$ scores ($-1.49$ versus $-1.54$) is an indication that jackknife inferences may be slightly liberal in terms of Type I error.

Like the bootstrap, the jackknife has been used primarily as an alternative inferential tool useful when the assumptions of traditional parametric inference do not apply. However, the jackknife has been shown to fail for markedly nonlinear statistics such as the sample median, unlike the bootstrap (Efron, 1982, p. 9). But although the bootstrap outstrips the jackknife in its generality because of this quality, there is evidence that the jackknife may be superior to the bootstrap in the area of complex sampling. When the sampling structure is known, it appears that one can develop reliable estimates of linear sample statistics by setting up the $g$ subsamples for jackknifing to parallel the strata and clusters of the sample (Fay, 1985).

Another use of the jackknife is in the identification of influential cases or strata in a statistical model, much like Cook's (1977) $D$ statistic. When a subsample is either a single case or a meaningful group of cases such as a sample stratum, its pseudovalue can be used to assess whether that subgroup has a greater-than-average effect on the overall $\hat{\theta}$ than other subgroups. If one $\theta_{-1}$ is in some sense extraordinarily larger or smaller than the other $\theta_{-1}$'s (e.g., in terms of the number of standard errors it is away from $\hat{\theta}$), we may wish to check that case or stratum for measurement error, and/or for any indication that our model may be in

TABLE 1.4
Jackknifing the Mean of the Simulated Data From Table 1.1

| Case | Original Sample | $\hat{\theta}_{-1}$ | $\tilde{\theta}_g$ |
|------|-----------------|---------------------|---------------------|
| 1 | 0.697 | −0.315 | 0.675 |
| 2 | −1.395 | −0.243 | −1.413 |
| 3 | 1.408 | −0.340 | 1.400 |
| 4 | 0.875 | −0.322 | 0.878 |
| 5 | −2.039 | −0.221 | −2.051 |
| 6 | −0.727 | −0.266 | −0.746 |
| 7 | −0.366 | −0.279 | −0.369 |
| 8 | 2.204 | −0.367 | 2.183 |
| 9 | 0.179 | −0.298 | 0.182 |
| 10 | 0.261 | −0.300 | 0.240 |
| 11 | 1.099 | −0.329 | 1.081 |
| 12 | −0.787 | −0.264 | −0.804 |
| 13 | −0.097 | −0.288 | −0.108 |
| 14 | −1.779 | −0.230 | −1.790 |
| 15 | −0.152 | −0.286 | −0.166 |
| 16 | −1.768 | −0.230 | −1.790 |
| 17 | −0.016 | −0.291 | −0.021 |
| 18 | 0.587 | −0.312 | 0.588 |
| 19 | −0.270 | −0.282 | −0.282 |
| 20 | −0.101 | −0.288 | −0.108 |
| 21 | −1.415 | −0.243 | −1.413 |
| 22 | −0.860 | −0.262 | −0.862 |
| 23 | −1.234 | −0.249 | −1.239 |
| 24 | −0.457 | −0.276 | −0.456 |
| 25 | −0.133 | −0.287 | −0.137 |
| 26 | −1.583 | −0.237 | −1.587 |
| 27 | −0.914 | −0.260 | −0.920 |
| 28 | −1.121 | −0.253 | −1.123 |
| 29 | 0.739 | −0.317 | 0.733 |
| 30 | 0.714 | −0.316 | 0.704 |
| Mean | −0.282 | — | −0.291 |
| St. dev. | 1.039 | — | 1.038 |

$\hat{\theta} = \bar{X} = -0.282$
$\bar{\theta} = g^{-1}\Sigma\tilde{\theta}_g = -0.291$
Estimate(BIAS $\hat{\theta}$) = $\bar{\theta} - \hat{\theta} = -0.009$
Jackknifed $t$ score = $-1.540$
Parametric $t$ score = $\bar{X}/\hat{\sigma}_{\bar{X}} = -1.49$

error. The bootstrap cannot be used in this way because of the random nature of the generation of the resamples used to calculate the $\hat{\theta}^*$'s.

The jackknife is of largely historical interest today, except perhaps in the areas of complex sampling and influential case detection. But because it is historically prior to, but less general than, the bootstrap, it sheds some additional light on the main topic of this monograph. Like the bootstrap, the jackknife both was developed in response to the restrictions imposed by traditional parametric inference and substituted a much larger number of computations for the analytics and assumptions of the parametric approach. But unlike the bootstrap, the jackknife was developed by researchers who failed to depart completely from traditional parametric thinking, especially regarding the estimation of confidence intervals. By merely transforming the $\hat{\theta}$ into a statistic that is distributed as $t$, Tukey's use of the jackknife is merely a "patching up" of traditional parametric inference. $\hat{\theta}$ (or its transform) is still assumed to be distributed in some known way to which we compare our sample for a hypothesis test. Although the jackknife makes some use of the empirical sample variation to make inferences to $\theta$, it fails to take full advantage of this sample information. It remained for the bootstrap to take that final leap from estimating points on a standard sampling distribution imposed by assumption to developing a strictly empirical estimate of the entire sampling distribution of $\hat{\theta}$.

## Monte Carlo Evaluation of the Bootstrap

In the remainder of this monograph, we will show how the bootstrapped sampling distribution of $\hat{\theta}$ can be used to make inferences about $\theta$. But, as the bootstrap is so foreign to most social scientists schooled in the traditional parametric approach to inference, we will also engage in some limited, but suggestive, empirical evaluation of the procedure. In this way, we will not only show how to use the bootstrap to make inferences, but also demonstrate how well it performs under certain conditions. Our approach to this demonstration will be first to conduct a simulation experiment contrasting inferential techniques in the circumstance under consideration, and then to provide a real-data example of bootstrapping in that circumstance, just as was done above on the sample mean and OLS regression estimates.

We use Monte Carlo simulation experiments in the following manner to study the bootstrap's performance (Sobol, 1975, chap. 1). First, a "population" is defined by a random number generating process. Second, a sample with specific characteristics is drawn using this random

28

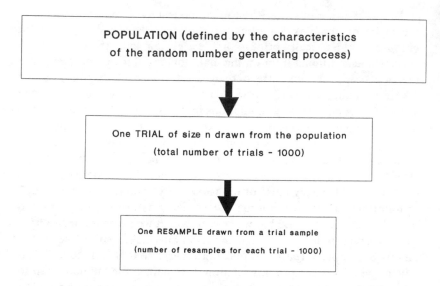

Figure 1.10. Nested Resampling for Monte Carlo Evaluation of the Bootstrap

process. This is the original sample for the first *trial*. From this sample, a statistic ($\hat{\theta}_t^S$) is calculated and stored, where the superscript S denotes that it is developed from an original sample and the subscript $t$ indicates the trial number. This $\hat{\theta}_t^S$ is then bootstrapped to yield the estimate of its sampling distribution, $\hat{F}^*(\hat{\theta}^*)$. Estimates of the inferential parameters of interest (confidence interval endpoints and bias estimates, as described in Chapter 2) are then computed for $\hat{\theta}_t^S$ using both parametric and bootstrap methods. This entire procedure, from generating the sample to estimating the inferential statistics, is repeated 1,000 times.[12] All this sampling, resampling, and computation finally yields a Monte Carlo generated frequency distribution for each of these inferential statistics. These are then used to evaluate each inferential approach. These multiple layers of Monte Carlo estimation and statistical development are depicted in Figure 1.10. This procedure is one of the only ways of evaluating the accuracy of an inferential technique, as it allows the researcher knowledge of the true population parameter, something real-data examples do not. Monte Carlo simulation has been used widely to evaluate and elucidate statistical procedures (Anderson, 1976; Duval & Groeneveld, 1987; Everitt, 1980; Hanushek & Jackson, 1977; Jolliffe, 1972).

This procedure yields two types of information useful in evaluating the bootstrap. First, a Monte Carlo estimate of the true sampling distribution of $\hat{\theta}$ can be constructed by developing a relative frequency distribution of the 1,000 $\hat{\theta}_r^S$'s, one from each trial. Recall that in bootstrapping we develop a Monte Carlo estimate of $F(\hat{\theta})$ using the sample, because we do not have complete information about the population. In these simulations, we know the population characteristics, and we can use this knowledge to get a very sound estimate of $F(\hat{\theta})$.

The second type of information that we can get from this simulation experiment is a Monte Carlo estimate of the distribution of the inferential statistics we are interested in comparing—for example, the endpoints of a confidence interval. As these statistics are random variables, any single estimate of them will include a degree of random error. To appreciate the empirical properties of the estimator in general, as opposed to any individual estimate, we must examine its sampling distribution.

This information will then be used to evaluate and compare inferential techniques. One standard of comparison will be the Monte Carlo estimate of the sampling distribution of the original $\hat{\theta}$ of interest. For instance, consider the 2.5[th] percentile point in the sampling distribution of $\hat{\theta}$ (to be used as the lower endpoint of a .05 $\alpha$-level confidence interval). The Monte Carlo estimate of this point is simply the 25th-lowest value of the 1,000 $\hat{\theta}_r^S$'s. This standard can be compared to the expected value of the distributions of this endpoint generated by the various inferential approaches we will describe below. The closer this expected value is to the Monte Carlo estimate, the less bias there is in that method of inference. The inferential method with the 2.5[th] percentile point closest to that of the Monte Carlo estimate will be the one with the least bias. Further, the standard deviation of that confidence interval endpoint for each inferential method is an estimate of the efficiency of that method. Each method can therefore be evaluated as to its bias and efficiency in generating the inferential statistic of interest.

Confidence intervals generated in this way can also be used to evaluate the error rates of their corresponding hypothesis tests. We commit a Type I error when we reject a true null hypothesis or fail to include the true value of $\theta$ in a confidence interval.[13] The probability of committing such an error is conventionally denoted as $\alpha$ and fixed in parametric tests using the probabilities associated with assumed, standard sampling distributions. If this parametric assumption is violated, however, the true $\alpha$ level may differ from the nominal $\alpha$ level. In our evaluations, we assess the Monte Carlo estimate of the true $\alpha$ level for each confidence interval technique by reporting the proportion of trials that fail to capture the true value of the θ examined. As we will use a nominal α level of .05 throughout this monograph, the direction and magnitude of the true α level's deviation from .05 will be another indication of the accuracy of each approach.

## 2. STATISTICAL INFERENCE USING THE BOOTSTRAP

The purpose of estimating the sampling distribution of $\hat{\theta}$ is to make inferences about θ. Two complementary ways of doing this are the development of an estimate of the bias of $\hat{\theta}$ and the development of confidence intervals around θ, given $\hat{\theta}$. The latter use of the estimated sampling distribution of $\hat{\theta}$ is by far the most general, and the most complex, application of the bootstrap, but the former is sometimes useful as well.

### Bias Estimation

The bias of an estimator of θ is the difference between the expected value of that estimator and the true value of the parameter:

$$\text{Bias}(\hat{\theta}) = \theta - E(\hat{\theta}). \tag{9}$$

The question is, On average, is $\hat{\theta}$ correct? Does the sampling distribution of $\hat{\theta}$ center on θ? This is of course important to a researcher trying to make statements about the true value of a parameter. If a statistic is biased, and the researcher does not know the degree of that bias, it is difficult for him or her to make accurate inferences about θ. It may be the case that a biased statistic is still the best available estimator in a practical sense, especially if it has a small variance around its expected value. For example, in the case of severe multicollinearity in a regression model, without imposing a bit of bias on the regression coefficient estimates via ridge regression, it would be impossible to obtain estimates of these coefficients. Even in this case, however, it is important to understand how large that imposed bias is before making any statements about θ.

Many statistics have been proven to be asymptotically unbiased estimates of certain parameters, for example, the sample mean as an estimator of the population mean under certain conditions. But there are several situations where the unbiasedness of $\hat{\theta}$ should not be assumed. First, there are statistics that are known to be biased estimators of certain parameters. One example is the ratio of two sample means, $\hat{\mu}/\hat{\upsilon}$, as the estimate of the ratio of two population means, $\mu/\upsilon$ (Rao & Beegle, 1967). Likewise, the sample coefficient of determination, $R^2$, is biased upward as an estimator of the population parameter, $\rho^2$ (Barton, 1962). The adjusted $R^2$ tends to reduce the bias caused by increasing the number of parameters in a regression model, but it does not eliminate it entirely. And, as mentioned above, in ridge regression the analyst intentionally induces a small amount of bias into coefficient estimates in an effort to make these estimates more efficient than they would otherwise owing to multicollinearity (Mason & Brown, 1975).

An estimate of a statistic's bias might also be useful when a statistic has been proven unbiased under specific conditions, but might be biased when these conditions do not hold. For example, OLS regression coefficients will be biased if the model assumption of zero correlation between the error term and the exogenous variables is violated, and even small amounts of correlation here can cause problems (Bartels, 1991). Also, the standard errors of MLEs are biased estimators of the population standard deviations when the sample size is small. Considering the wide use of some of these estimators in the social sciences, an understanding of their bias may be important in certain circumstances, but traditional inferential statistics provides no general way to explore it.

The bootstrapped sampling distribution, $\hat{F}^*(\hat{\theta}^*)$, can be used to assess the bias of $\hat{\theta}$ in the following straightforward manner. Although $\hat{F}^*(\hat{\theta}^*)$ is itself not a completely unbiased estimate of $F(\hat{\theta})$, a good approximation of the bias of $\hat{\theta}$ is the difference between the expected value of the bootstrapped sampling distribution and $\hat{\theta}$ (Efron, 1982, p. 33):

$$\text{Estimate}[\text{Bias}(\hat{\theta})] = \hat{\theta} - \hat{\theta}^*_{(.)} \ , \qquad \text{where } \hat{\theta}^*_{(.)} = \sum \hat{\theta}_b / B. \quad (10)$$

That is, a bootstrapped estimate of the bias of $\hat{\theta}$ is simply the difference between the analytic point estimator and bootstrapped point estimate of that parameter, which is the average of the $B$ $\hat{\theta}^*$'s from the resamples.

In Table 2.1, we report the results of a 5,000-trial Monte Carlo experiment assessing the bootstrapped estimate of the bias of the ratio of two sample means as an estimator of the ratio of two population means. This table displays the expected values of the Monte Carlo and

TABLE 2.1

The Bias of the Ratio of Two Sample Means—Monte Carlo
Experiment Results

| | Monte Carlo | | Bootstrap | |
|---|---|---|---|---|
| | $E(\bar{X}/\bar{Y})^a$ | E (bias estimate) | $E(\bar{X}/\bar{Y})$ | E (bias estimate) |
| Normal variables, | | | | |
| $n = 50$ | .751 | 0.001 | .752 | 0.001 |
| Normal variables, | | | | |
| $n = 20$ | .752 | 0.002 | .755 | 0.002 |
| Log-normal variables, | | | | |
| $n = 50$ | .930 | 0.025 | .956 | 0.026 |
| Log-normal variables, | | | | |
| $n = 20$ | .983 | 0.078 | 1.039 | 0.057 |

NOTE: $B = 1,000$; number of trials = 5,000.
a. True ratios-normal variables, .75; log-normal variables, .90.

bootstrap estimates of this ratio, as well as their estimates of the bias of
this statistic under four conditions. The Monte Carlo bias estimate was
derived for each trial by subtracting $\hat{\theta}$ from the true $\theta$ (known from the
random number generating process), and the bootstrapped estimate was
derived by subtracting the bootstrapped estimate, $\hat{\theta}^*$, from $\hat{\theta}$ for each trial.

As can be seen, the bootstrapped bias estimate performs quite well in
each of these cases. The bootstrapped bias estimates are both in the same
direction and of the same magnitude as the Monte Carlo estimates.
When the two variables whose means are compared are normally distributed, the bias is small and the bootstrapped estimate is exactly the
same as the Monte Carlo estimate. When the variables are log-normally
distributed, the bias is increased, especially with a small sample, but the
bootstrap still provides a reasonable estimate of that bias.

The importance of estimating $\hat{\theta}$'s bias in this instance is apparent from
this experiment, as well, in that the difference between the true and
estimated ratio of means is quite significant in some cases. For example,
in the case of a sample size of 20 with log-normal variables, the true
ratio is .90, but the expected value of the standard estimator is around
.98. Another important point that this analysis raises is that one should
take care in using the bootstrapped point estimate of a biased statistic.
The same property that allows the assessment of bias using the bootstrap
(i.e., mirroring the bias of a statistic) serves to exacerbate the bias of

the bootstrap estimate. The bootstrap is therefore useful for developing inferences to populations, but not necessarily for developing point estimates of parameters.

Although it may be tempting simply to subtract this bootstrap estimate of $\hat{\theta}$'s bias from the sample $\hat{\theta}$ in an attempt to achieve an unbiased estimate of $\theta$, this is generally not a good idea. The bootstrap bias estimator from a single sample contains an indeterminate amount of random variability along with bias, and this may artificially inflate the mean squared error of $\hat{\theta}$ (Hinckley, 1978). But the bias estimate is useful in determining if there is a serious bias problem in our estimate of $\theta$. Whether a given level of bias is a problem or not depends upon the empirical situation at hand, of course. However, we are often concerned about whether the bias in a statistic is significantly large compared with its standard deviation. If the standard deviation is much greater than the bias, we may be comfortable in disregarding the latter, as the random error will therefore overwhelm it. Efron (1982, p. 8) suggests that when the ratio of the estimated bias to the standard error is less than .25, the bias of $\hat{\theta}$ is not usually a serious problem. The bootstrap provides a general method of estimating this ratio that traditional approaches do not.

## Bootstrap Confidence Intervals

The development of confidence intervals around population parameters (and the parallel tests of hypotheses) is the most common method of using an estimate of a statistic's sampling distribution to make inferences. An $\alpha$-level confidence interval is defined as those values of $\hat{\theta}$ an analyst feels $[(1 - \alpha) \times 100]\%$ certain will include the true value of $\theta$, given the variability in the sample and the shape of $\hat{\theta}$'s sampling distribution. It is the shape of $F(\hat{\theta})$ that is crucial here.

Traditional parametric confidence intervals begin with an assumption about the shape of $F(\hat{\theta})$, for example, that it is normal or Student's $t$ shaped. The parameters of this assumed distribution are then estimated analytically from the sample, yielding an implicit estimate of $F(\hat{\theta})$, as discussed in Chapter 1. The $\alpha/2$ and the $1 - \alpha/2$ percentile points in this distribution are selected as the upper and lower endpoints of an $\alpha$-level confidence interval around $\theta$. The traditional interpretation of this confidence interval is that it contains most of the values of $\theta$ that could have generated the random sample of size $n$, given the data at hand.[14] We allow for the possibility of not including the true value of $\theta$ into the interval, expecting that $(\alpha \times 100)\%$ of the time this will happen by chance. But the values within the confidence interval are not far enough away from $\hat{\theta}$ to be rejected as unequal to $\theta$, at a nominal $\alpha$ level of confidence.

Consider the familiar example of a .05 $\alpha$-level confidence interval around a population mean, $\mu$. The sample mean, $\overline{X}$, is typically assumed to be normally distributed around $\mu$ for $n > 30$. The standard normal ($z$) or Student's $t$ table can give us the probability of randomly drawing a sample yielding an $\overline{X}_i$ that lies a given number of standard deviations away from the expected value of $\overline{X}$'s sampling distribution, which is $\mu$ because $\overline{X}$ is an unbiased estimator. For example, chances are 1 in 20 that we would draw an $\overline{X}_i$ that is 1.645 standard deviations greater than the population mean if $F(\overline{X})$ is normal. We can select the endpoints of an $\alpha$-level confidence interval around $\mu$ by converting the $z$ score corresponding to our acceptable level of risk of Type I error by multiplying it by the standard deviation of that mean in the familiar way:

$$p(\overline{X} - z_{\alpha/2}\sigma_{\overline{X}} < \mu < \overline{X} + z_{\alpha/2}\sigma_{\overline{X}}) = 1 - \alpha. \qquad (11)$$

The resulting confidence interval can be interpreted as the values we can be $[(1 - \alpha) \times 100]\%$ certain include the true value of $\theta$, given our sample and given that our assumption about the shape of the sampling distribution of $\hat{\theta}$ is correct.

As noted above, however, this assumption regarding the shape of the sampling distribution of $\hat{\theta}$ may not be correct. We may not be entirely confident that the conditions allowing for the assumption of a known distribution in fact hold, or we may be working with a statistic without any sampling distribution theory. In such cases, the traditional methods fail, and the bootstrap may be helpful.

Over the past decade, substantial attention has been paid to the theoretical development of techniques using the bootstrap sampling distribution, $\hat{F}^*(\hat{\theta}^*)$, to build confidence intervals around various population parameters.[15] This monograph describes and demonstrates the four bootstrap confidence interval techniques that are the most general and practical for the social scientist: the normal approximation method, the percentile method, the bias-corrected percentile (BC) method, and the percentile-$t$ method.

The *normal approximation method* is quite analogous to the parametric approach to constructing confidence intervals (Noreen, 1989, p. 69).

When it is plausible to assume a statistic is normally distributed, but no analytic standard error formula exists for it, the bootstrapped sampling distribution can be used to estimate that standard error. This may be quite useful, for example, for complex MLEs with singular information matrices. This estimation is a straightforward application of the notion that the $\hat{\theta}^*$'s are random variables distributed as $\hat{\theta}$:

$$\hat{\sigma}_{\hat{\theta}}^* = \left[\left(\sum [\hat{\theta}_b^* - \hat{\theta}_{(.)}^*]^2\right)/(B-1)\right]^{1/2}, \quad \text{where } \hat{\theta}_{(.)}^* = \sum \hat{\theta}_b^* / B. \quad (12)$$

As Efron (1981b) shows, as $B \to \infty$, $\hat{\sigma}_{\hat{\theta}}^* \to \hat{\sigma}_{\hat{\theta}}$, but little improvement in the approximation occurs as $B$ exceeds 50-200 (Efron & Tibshirani, 1986, sec. 9).

Just as in the traditional parametric case, we identify the points on the $z$ or Student's $t$ distribution associated with $\alpha/2$ and $1 - \alpha/2$. We then use the bootstrapped standard error, $\hat{\sigma}_{\hat{\theta}}^*$, to transform these $z$ and $t$ scores into the metric of the sample, by inserting it into the traditional confidence interval formula:

$$p(\hat{\theta} - z_{\alpha/2}\hat{\sigma}_{\hat{\theta}}^* < \theta < \hat{\theta} + z_{\alpha/2}\hat{\sigma}_{\hat{\theta}}^*) = 1 - \alpha. \quad (13)$$

Consider the data regarding the sample mean first generated in Table 1.1. Table 1.2 shows that the standard deviation of the bootstrapped sample mean is extremely close to that calculated analytically from the original sample. Therefore, the confidence interval endpoints developed using the normal approximation and parametric methods will be virtually identical in this case. Again, this is as we would expect given that the mean in this case is probably normally distributed.

Historically, the general idea behind the normal approximation was the first application of the bootstrap and related techniques in inferential statistics (e.g., Efron, 1979, 1982, chap. 5; Tukey, 1958), and its appeal to those trained in the traditional approach is clear. It makes use of an assumption (normality) and a set of tables (the $z$ and $t$ tables) with which all applied researchers are familiar. When the assumption of normality for $\hat{\theta}$ is justified, these confidence intervals may in fact be more accurate than those developed without this parametric restriction. If we have sound prior information about the shape of $F(\hat{\theta})$, we certainly should use it. The generation of standard deviations and the assumption of $\hat{F}^*(\hat{\theta}^*)$'s normality also allow for the development of hypothesis tests regarding $\theta$. It should also be noted that the normal approximation method typically requires many fewer bootstrap replications than the other bootstrap confidence interval techniques described below (Efron & Tibshirani, 1986, sec. 9).

The chief problem with the normal approximation method is that it fails to take full advantage of the property that $\hat{F}^*(\hat{\theta}^*)$ estimates the *whole* sampling distribution of $\hat{\theta}$, not just its second moment. The bootstrap was designed to be a nonparametric technique, and normal approximation confidence intervals clearly rely on a strong parametric assumption. Although this assumption may sometimes be justified, confidence intervals developed in this way are no better than those developed with the parametric approach when this particular assumption is violated.

The *percentile method,* on the other hand, takes literally the notion that $\hat{F}^*(\hat{\theta}^*)$ approximates $F(\hat{\theta})$. The basic approach is extremely simple: An $\alpha$-level confidence interval includes all the values of $\hat{\theta}^*$ between the $\alpha/2$ and $1 - \alpha/2$ percentiles of the $\hat{F}^*(\hat{\theta}^*)$ distribution (Efron, 1982, chap. 10; Stine, 1990, pp. 249-250). That is, the endpoints of a .05 $\alpha$-level confidence interval for $\hat{\theta}$ would be the values of $\hat{\theta}^*$ at the $2.5^{th}$ and $97.5^{th}$ percentile of $\hat{F}^*(\hat{\theta}^*)$. A sorted vector of $\hat{\theta}^*$'s allows for the easy development of such a confidence interval. Consider again our initial example of bootstrapping a sample mean in Tables 1.1 and 1.2. Given that $B = 1,000$, we simply count up to the 25th-lowest value of $\overline{X}^*$, and count down to the 25th-highest value. This yields a confidence interval for $\mu$ of

$$p(-.6544 < \mu < .0910) = .95.$$

Clearly, this interval is very similar to that developed using the standard method in Table 1.2. Again, this is as expected, because the assumption of normality for $F(\overline{X})$ is justified in this case, and so the parametric interval is likely to be correct.

The percentile method frees the researcher from the parametric assumption of both the traditional and normal approximation techniques. If a statistic is distributed asymmetrically, for example, it does not in theory adversely affect the accuracy of the percentile method's confidence interval. Consider the sample mean of a skewed and truncated variable (e.g., annual state oil production) where the sample size is 20. The central limit theorem justifies the assumption of normality for $\overline{X}$

when $n$ is large (conventionally, when $n > 30$) or when the underlying variable is normally distributed, but neither of these conditions holds here. And recall that Figure 1.4 indicated that such a situation would yield an asymmetric sampling distribution for $\overline{X}$. The traditional parametric estimate of $F(\overline{X})$ would be inappropriate in this case, and therefore the confidence interval endpoints derived from it would be inaccurate. But the bootstrap percentile method allows $\hat{F}^*(\hat{\theta}^*)$ to conform to any shape the data suggest. This allows confidence intervals to be asymmetrical around the expected value of $\hat{\theta}$.

The percentile method also has the advantage of being simple to execute. We need no complex analytical formulas to estimate the parameters of $\hat{\theta}$'s assumed sampling distribution, and no tabled values for the probabilities of the points on the standardized sampling distribution. We need only calculate the $\hat{\theta}^*$'s, sort them, and count up and down to the appropriate percentiles. Further, the percentile method is quite intuitive, once one accepts the bootstrapping principle. We have an estimate of $F(\hat{\theta})$ and we simply pluck off the appropriate percentile points. For these reasons, it appears to be the most widely used bootstrap technique among applied statisticians (Liu & Singh, 1988, p. 978).

The percentile method has at least two drawbacks, however. First, as DiCiccio and Romano (1988) suggest, it may perform poorly with small samples, primarily because of the importance of the tails of the sampling distribution in these confidence interval calculations. It may be that larger samples are needed to flesh out these tails adequately. The second potential problem with the percentile method is that we must assume that the bootstrapped sampling distribution is an unbiased estimate of $F(\hat{\theta})$. Although this is certainly less restrictive than assuming $F(\hat{\theta})$ has some standard distribution with known properties, it may still cause concern. A further, if minor, inconvenience for the percentile compared with the normal approximation method is that one should generate and analyze at least 1,000 resamples for the former, whereas the latter may be accomplished with only 50-200 resamples. Given the availability and speed of modern computers, however, this is not usually a crucial consideration. The exception here could be for extremely complicated or otherwise computationally expensive statistics, such as order statistics with large samples (e.g., the median), and iteratively estimated statistics (e.g., MLEs).

In order to overcome the restriction of assuming unbiasedness for $\hat{F}^*(\hat{\theta}^*)$, Efron (1982, sec. 10.7) suggests a simple adjustment, the *bias-corrected* or *BC method*.[16] Instead of requiring that $\hat{\theta}^* - \hat{\theta}$, and $\hat{\theta} - \theta$

be centered on zero (that is, that $\hat{\theta}^*$ and $\hat{\theta}$ are unbiased estimators of $\hat{\theta}$ and $\theta$, respectively), the BC method assumes that these quantities are distributed around a constant, $z_0\sigma$, where $\sigma$ is the standard deviation of the respective distribution. This quantity, $z_0$, is a biasing constant for which we need to adjust the bootstrapped distribution of $\hat{\theta}$.

To make this adjustment, we assume that there exists some monotonic transformation of $\hat{\theta}$ and 0, say, $\hat{\varphi}$ and $\varphi$, respectively, whose differences are normally distributed[17] and centered on $z_0\sigma$:

$$\hat{\varphi} - \varphi \sim N(z_0\sigma, \sigma^2), \text{ and } \hat{\varphi}^* - \hat{\varphi} \sim N(z_0\sigma, \sigma^2). \qquad (14)$$

The quantity $\hat{\varphi} - \varphi$ is therefore a normal pivotal quantity with the same distribution under $F(\hat{\theta})$ and $\hat{F}^*(\hat{\theta}^*)$. This form of transformation of a statistic for mathematical tractability is not unusual. An example is Fisher's transformation of the correlation coefficient, $\tanh^{-1}\rho$. The interesting aspect of the use of this device in the BC method is that because the bootstrapped distribution $\hat{F}^*(\hat{\theta}^*)$ is invariant to transformation, we do not need to know the specific transformation function, only that such a function exists. Needing only to make the assumption that such a function exists is a much weaker requirement than actually having to calculate it.

By assuming the possibility of a normal transformation of this sort, we can calculate the value of $z_0$ using the cumulative normal distribution. Once we have estimated this constant, we merely have to adjust $\hat{F}^*(\hat{\theta}^*)$ to compensate for it.

The process of developing a BC confidence interval thus involves two steps: calculating $z_0$ and then using $z_0$ to adjust the bootstrapped sampling distribution. First, $z_0$ is the $z$ value corresponding to the proportion of $\hat{\theta}^*$'s that are less than or equal to $\hat{\theta}$, the original point estimator:

$$z_0 = \Phi^{-1}\{pr(\hat{\theta}^* \le \hat{\theta})\}, \qquad (15)$$

where $\Phi$ = the cumulative distribution function for the standard normal variable.

The endpoints of the BC interval are then found by adjusting the percentile values of $\hat{\theta}^*$ by the use of $z_0$ (Efron, 1982, sec. 10.7; Stine, 1990, p. 277):

$$\text{Lower BC endpoint} = \text{the value of the } \hat{\theta}^* \qquad (16)$$

$$\text{at the } [\{\Phi(2z_0 + z_{\alpha/2})\} \times 100] \text{ percentile;}$$

Upper BC endpoint = the value of the $\hat{\theta}^*$          (17)

at the $[\{\Phi(2z_0 + z_{1-\alpha/2})\} \times 100]$ percentile.

That is, we add twice the value of $z_0$ to the $z$ value associated with the nominal $\alpha/2$ level for each end of the confidence interval. We then find the probability associated with that adjusted $z$ value from a standard normal table. The value of $\hat{\theta}^*$ at the percentile value corresponding to this adjusted $z$ value is the BC confidence interval endpoint.

The BC method thus adjusts the bootstrapped sampling distribution to center on the point estimator, $\hat{\theta}$. If the distribution is already centered on this value, no adjustment is needed and the BC method endpoints will be the same as the percentile method endpoints. That is, if $\mathrm{pr}(\hat{\theta}^* \leq \hat{\theta}) = .5$, then $z_0 = \Phi^{-1}(.5) = 0$, so $\Phi(2z_0 + z_{\alpha/2}) = \alpha/2$. However, if $\mathrm{pr}(\hat{\theta}^* \leq \hat{\theta}) \neq .5$, that is, if the bootstrapped sampling distribution is not centered on $\hat{\theta}$, the BC endpoints will be corrected for this bias.

Consider the situation where $\mathrm{pr}(\hat{\theta}^* \leq \hat{\theta}) = .65$, because $E(\hat{\theta}^*) < \hat{\theta}$. Therefore if $\alpha = .05$,

$$z_0 = \Phi^{-1}(.65) = .39.$$

Upper BC endpoint percentile $= \Phi(2[.39] + 1.96) \times 100$

$\qquad\qquad\qquad\qquad\qquad = \Phi(2.74) \times 100$

$\qquad\qquad\qquad\qquad\qquad = 99.7^{\text{th}}$ percentile of $\hat{F}^*(\hat{\theta}^*)$

and

Lower BC endpoint percentile $= \Phi(2[.39] - 1.96) \times 100$

$\qquad\qquad\qquad\qquad\qquad = \Phi(-1.18) \times 100$

$\qquad\qquad\qquad\qquad\qquad = 11.9^{\text{th}}$ percentile of $\hat{F}^*(\hat{\theta}^*)$.

As this example shows, the nonlinear nature of the relationship between a $z$ score and its probability results in the upper and lower endpoints being shifted at unequal rates. The upper endpoint in this example shifted up only 2.2 percentiles, whereas the lower endpoint shifted up 9.4 percentiles. This means that the length of the BC confidence intervals may well be different from those of the percentile method, but the true $\alpha$ level may be closer to the nominal.

The chief problem with the BC method is that we need to resort to certain parametric assumptions. First, we must assume that there exists some monotonic transformation of $\hat{\theta}$ and $\theta$ whose differences have a known distribution, such as normality. Although this is certainly a much weaker requirement than actually finding this transformation, or assuming that $\hat{\theta}$ itself has some standard distribution, it still puts restrictions on the model. Further, we must assume that $\hat{\theta}$ is an unbiased estimator of $\theta$, as opposed to assuming $E(\hat{\theta}^*)$ is unbiased. That is, when these two quantities are not equal, the BC method gives the benefit of the doubt to $\hat{\theta}$, and this may or may not be justified in a given situation.

There has been some discussion in the bootstrapping literature, both theoretical (Babu & Singh, 1983; DiCiccio & Romano, 1988; Singh, 1981) and empirical (Hall, 1988b, p. 929; Loh & Wu, 1987), that the percentile method and its variants (e.g., the BC) are less than optimal uses of $\hat{F}^*(\hat{\theta}^*)$, however. Although simple and intuitive, the percentile methods may give inaccurate endpoints for confidence intervals because they concentrate on a quantity, $\hat{\theta}^*$, that is not necessarily a pivotal of $\hat{F}$ (Babu & Singh, 1983; DiCiccio & Romano, 1988; Hinckley, 1988, p. 326). This can be a problem, especially for a statistic with a skewed sampling distribution (Hall, 1988b, sec. 3; Singh, 1986).

The *percentile-t method* has been proposed as a way to correct for this problem (Bickel & Freedman, 1981; Efron, 1981b, sec. 9). Here we transform $\hat{\theta}^*$ into a standardized variable, $t^*$:

$$t_b^* = (\hat{\theta}_b^* - \hat{\theta})/\hat{\sigma}_{\hat{\theta}} . \tag{18}$$

These $t^*$'s are distributed as $\hat{\theta}$, but on a standardized scale. This standardized bootstrap distribution of the estimator is used to develop the critical points in the sampling distribution of $\hat{\theta}$ in a way completely analogous to the use of the Student's $t$ distributions in parametric inference. In the percentile-$t$ method, we determine the $\alpha/2$ and $1 - \alpha/2$ percentile values of $t^*$ and develop a confidence interval around $\theta$ as follows:

$$p(\hat{\theta} - t_{\alpha/2}^* \hat{\sigma}_{\hat{\theta}} < \theta < \hat{\theta} + t_{1-\alpha/2}^* \hat{\sigma}_{\hat{\theta}}) = 1 - \alpha , \tag{19}$$

using $\hat{\sigma}_{\hat{\theta}}$ calculated from the original sample, whether analytically or through bootstrapping, as in Equation 12.

A key issue is how to estimate $\hat{\sigma}_{\hat{\theta}}$ to convert the $\hat{\theta}^*$'s to $t^*$'s (Equation 18). Though several suggestions are offered in the literature (e.g., Bickel & Freedman, 1981; Hinckley, 1988), we believe that $\hat{\theta}_b^*$ needs to be converted to $t_b^*$ using an estimate of $\hat{\sigma}_{\hat{\theta}}$ derived from each resample. This will weight each $\hat{\theta}^*$ based on the confidence we have in it, shifting the $\hat{\theta}^*$'s with small standard deviations toward the center of $\hat{F}^*(\hat{\theta}^*)$ and those with large standard deviations toward the tails. Therefore, one must calculate not only $\hat{\theta}_b^*$ from each resample, but also an estimate of $\hat{\sigma}_{\hat{\theta}}$. This estimation may be done analytically, if such a formula exists for $\hat{\sigma}_{\hat{\theta}}$, or it may be calculated by conducting another round of bootstrapping (Equation 12), yielding $\hat{\sigma}_{\hat{\theta}}^*$. This "double bootstrap" involves another level of resampling, so that one is actually resampling from a resample.

The double bootstrap is the most general approach to the percentile-$t$, but it will clearly increase the overall computational effort by a factor of the number of "re-resamples" one undertakes to determine $\hat{\sigma}_{\hat{\theta}}^*$ in each resample. This should be 50-200, as suggested in our discussion of Equation 12. That is, to develop a percentile-$t$ confidence interval around some $\theta$ with 1,000 resamples, we would need to draw 200,000 samples (1,000 resamples from the original data, and 200 re-resamples apiece from each of these resamples for the calculation of the $\hat{\sigma}_{\hat{\theta}}^*$'s). Again, this level of computation may be of special concern when a statistic requires a great deal of calculation, for example, a sample median or an MLE. This increase in computational effort may be justified if the percentile-$t$ is highly accurate (Hall, 1988b, p. 929; Hinckley, 1988; Loh & Wu, 1987). And of course, if computational capacity is a concern, an analyst would be unlikely to opt for the bootstrap over parametric methods in the first place.

Other procedures for developing bootstrap confidence intervals have been suggested (e.g., DiCiccio & Romano, 1989; Efron, 1981a, 1987), but the four described in detail here—the normal approximation, the percentile, the BC, and the percentile-$t$—appear to be the ones that best take advantage of bootstrapping's benefits. They are automatic and relatively simple to program, they are easy to understand conceptually, and they can be applied to perhaps any statistic developed from a simple random sample (Efron & Gong, 1983; Tibshirani, 1988).[18] For these reasons, they are the leading candidates for application in the social sciences.

The choice of which bootstrap confidence interval method to use is highly dependent on the practical research situation facing an analyst. None of these techniques offers the best confidence intervals in every situation, because the criteria for judging the quality of their results vary

TABLE 2.2
A Comparison of Bootstrap Confidence Interval Methods

| Method | Advantages | Disadvantages |
|---|---|---|
| Normal approximation | similar to the familiar parametric approach; useful with a normally distributed $\hat{\theta}$; requires the least computation ($B = 50$-$200$) | fails to use the entire $\hat{F}^*(\hat{\theta}^*)$; requires parametric assumption about $F(\hat{\theta})$ |
| Percentile | uses the entire $\hat{F}^*(\hat{\theta}^*)$; allows $F(\hat{\theta})$ to be asymmetrical; invariant to transformation | small samples may result in low accuracy; assumes $\hat{F}^*(\hat{\theta}^*)$ to be unbiased |
| BC | all of those of the percentile method; allows for bias in $\hat{F}^*(\hat{\theta}^*)$; $z_0$ can be calculated easily from $\hat{F}^*(\hat{\theta}^*)$ | requires a limited parametric assumption |
| Percentile-$t$ | highly accurate confidence intervals in many cases; handles skewed $F(\hat{\theta})$ better than the percentile method | not invariant to transformation; computationally expensive with the double bootstrap |

widely (DiCiccio & Romano, 1988). For example, if a researcher is concerned with minimizing computational expenditure, the normal approximation is the best option. On the other hand, if maximizing the accuracy of the hypothesis test is crucial, the percentile-$t$ method might be preferable. Also, the nature of the population parameter and estimator under consideration will affect the choice of method. For example, one might be willing to assume $F(\hat{\theta})$ is normally distributed for some $\theta$, and therefore opt for the normal approximation method, but one might not be willing to make such an assumption for some other statistic and so would need to use a different method. Table 2.2 summarizes some of the strong and weak points of each method.

# 3. APPLICATIONS OF BOOTSTRAP CONFIDENCE INTERVALS

The bootstrap is designed to be a handy, widely applicable, and practical technique for making statistical inferences. Researchers in a variety of social scientific disciplines have found it to be useful in studying topics as diverse as peak electricity demand (Al-Sahlawi, 1990; Veall, 1987), stereotypic love (Borrello & Thompson, 1989), the French macro-economy (Bianchi, Calzolari, & Brillet, 1987), and even the inflation rate for alcoholic beverage prices (Selvanathan, 1989).

In this chapter, we examine statistical situations where the bootstrap may have some advantages over traditional parametric inference. In some cases, this is because certain assumptions of the traditional approach are violated. In other cases, there simply exist no justifiable parametric methods to apply. Our approach is to describe a general statistical situation and then discuss why the bootstrap might be preferable to the parametric approach. We then conduct a Monte Carlo experiment (see Chapter 1) on each situation, comparing the performance of the various confidence intervals, and use examples of actual social scientific data that illustrate the general situations we discuss.

## Confidence Intervals for
## Statistics With Unknown Sampling Distributions

As discussed in Chapter 1, in order to make inferences from a sample statistic to a population parameter, an analyst needs to be able to estimate the sampling distribution of that statistic. The traditional parametric approach is to use prior information about the shape of this distribution and analytic formulas to estimate it in a given case. For example, we have good reason to believe that the sample mean for $n = 50$ is normally distributed, and we can use this information in conjunction with sample data to estimate $F(\overline{X})$ for a given statistical situation.

Many practicing social scientists take for granted that they know the shapes of the distributions of the statistics they use. The central limit theorem assures us of the normality of certain commonly used statistics as sample size increases, and certain other known distributions (such as the $\chi^2$, $F$, and Student's $t$) are known for other statistics. And further, simple analytic formulas to estimate the parameters of these distributions are also available in many cases. For example, the mean and standard error formulas for many of the normally distributed statistics we commonly use (e.g., the sample mean, the difference between two sample means, and OLS regression coefficients) are well known and thoroughly discussed in introductory statistics texts.

There are, however, many statistics that might be of interest to social scientists that have unknown sampling distributions, no analytic formulas available for the parameters of these sampling distributions, and/or formulas that are intractable in certain cases. The list of such statistics to which the bootstrap has been applied is long, and it grows monthly. These include skew and kurtosis estimators (Badrinath & Chatterjee, 1991), redundancy statistics (Lambert, Wildt, & Durand, 1989), Angoff's delta item bias index (Harris & Kolen, 1989), the constant term of a Cobb-Douglas translog multiplicative model (Srivastava & Singh, 1989), eigenvalues (Lambert, Wildt, & Durand, 1990), and the switch point in a switching regression model (Douglas, 1987).

## *The Sample Mean From a Small Sample*

Among the most common estimators used in the social sciences is the sample mean, $\overline{X} = \Sigma x_i/n$. If we want to describe the central tendency of a variable that is symmetrically distributed, we use the mean. An important characteristic of the sample mean is the central limit theorem, which holds that as sample size increases, the mean tends to have a normal sampling distribution, regardless of the distribution of the underlying variable. Typically, introductory statistics texts suggest that a sample size of 30 or more is "large enough" to invoke this theorem and assume a normal sampling distribution for $\overline{X}$ (e.g., Mansfield, 1986, p. 241). Further, even for samples of fewer than 20 or 30, it has been shown that if the underlying variable is normally distributed, then the mean will be normally distributed. Clearly, it seems that the sample mean is a statistic with one of the most well-grounded cases for using parametric inference.

There may be cases, however, where an analyst would like to make inferences to a population mean from a sample of fewer than 30 cases and where the assumption of the variable's normality is not justified. In such cases, we do not know the shape of $\overline{X}$'s sampling distribution. The assumption that this distribution is normal would not be justified, and could result in a greater than nominal error rate for a statistical test regarding $\mu$. The bootstrap could be used to make inferences in this case.

We have simulated a situation of this type with a sample size of 25 from a log-normal variable. Figure 3.1 shows a Monte Carlo simulation of the mean of such a sample. A K-S test indicates that this is not a normal distribution, and assuming that it is so could adversely affect our inferential error rate. Table 3.1 displays the results of a Monte Carlo experiment on parametric and bootstrap confidence intervals around the population mean, $\mu$, under these conditions. Several interesting findings

P(Value of Mean)

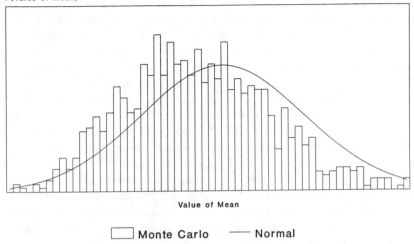

Value of Mean

☐ Monte Carlo    ——— Normal

Figure 3.1. Monte Carlo Simulated Versus Normal Sampling Distribution of the Mean of a Log-Normal Variable ($n = 25$)

NOTE: Normal distribution has the same mean and standard deviation as the Monte Carlo estimate.

TABLE 3.1

The Mean of a Log-Normal Variable—
Monte Carlo Experiment Results

|  | $\alpha/2$ Endpoint | $1 - \alpha/2$ Endpoint | Proportion of Type I Error ($\alpha$ level)[a] |
|---|---|---|---|
| Monte Carlo estimate | 0.627 | 1.427 | — |
| Parametric[b] | 0.600 (.141)[c] | 1.401 (.287) | .080 |
| Normal approximation[b] | 0.628 (.144) | 1.373 (.280) | .091 |
| Percentile | 0.655 (.141) | 1.404 (.291) | .084 |
| BC | 0.673 (.143) | 1.421 (.299) | .084 |
| Percentile-$t$ | 0.583 (.177) | 1.476 (.333) | .059 |

NOTE: Nominal $\alpha$ level = .05; $B = 1,000$; $n = 25$. Monte Carlo $\overline{X}$ = 1.00 (s.d. = .199); bootstrap $\overline{X}^*$ = 1.00 (s.d. = .190).
a. Proportion of the trials that the true value of $\mu$ was left out of the confidence interval. The true value of $\mu$ equals 1.00, as defined by the random number generator.
b. Using $t_{.025;df=24} = 2.064$ for both the parametric and normal approximation intervals.
c. Standard deviation of the confidence interval endpoint estimate.

emerge from this analysis. The single most important indicator of confidence interval quality is how closely the proportion of Type I errors matches the nominal $\alpha$ level (.05) used to construct these intervals. All of the intervals exclude the true value of $\mu$ too often; for example, the parametric confidence interval's $\alpha$ level is .08. Only the percentile-$t$ interval comes closer to the nominal $\alpha$ level than the parametric does, however, excluding $\mu$ 5.9% of the time. This means that each of these intervals underestimates the level of Type I error, but the percentile-$t$ is the most accurate. The percentile-$t$ has been touted as performing well in the face of a skewed sampling distribution (Hall, 1988b, sec. 3; Singh, 1986), and this experiment appears to confirm this, as the distribution displayed in Figure 3.1 is skewed.

Close examination of Table 3.1 reveals other interesting attributes of these intervals. First, the point estimates of the endpoints have different types and levels of bias. The parametric interval is shifted to the left at both endpoints in an approximately symmetric fashion. That is, both parametric endpoint estimators are about .027 less than the Monte Carlo estimates. The bootstrap estimates are asymmetric in their bias, reflecting the asymmetry in the sampling distribution of this $\overline{X}$. The degree of bias varies between bootstrap approaches and the estimated endpoint, however. For example, the normal approximation interval has an expected value for the lower endpoint almost exactly the same as the lower endpoint estimated through Monte Carlo simulation. The upper endpoint for the normal approximation is biased downward, however. The BC method has the best estimate for the upper endpoint, but the worst for the lower endpoint. This may indicate that the BC method does best in the long, thin tails of skewed sampling distributions, as in the right-hand tail of this $\overline{X}$'s sampling distribution. The efficiency of these endpoint estimators is also of interest. On each endpoint, the standard errors of each of the approaches' estimates are quite similar, except for the percentile-$t$. In this interval, we find somewhat more variation in the endpoint estimates. So, although the percentile-$t$ offers the best overall error rate, its intervals are somewhat less efficient in this example. Also, the efficiency of each interval approach is much better for the $\alpha/2$ endpoint than the $1 - \alpha/2$ endpoint. This is likely to be the result of the longer, thinner tail that is found in the upper end of this $\overline{X}$'s sampling distribution.

In Figure 3.2, we display the bootstrap sampling distribution of the mean 1985 state oil production for a sample of 20 states, a statistical situation similar to the Monte Carlo experiment. The comparison with

P(Value of Mean)

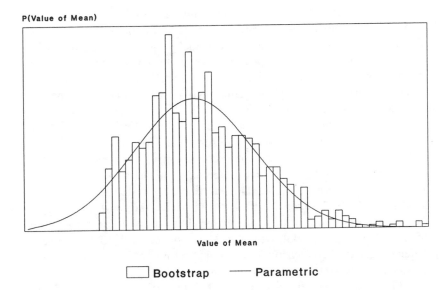

Value of Mean

☐ Bootstrap ——— Parametric

Figure 3.2. Bootstrap Versus Parametric Estimate of the Sampling Distribution
of 1985 Mean State Oil Production ($n = 20$)
SOURCE: Data from Dye and Taintor (1991).

the overlaid parametric distribution for this mean shows that the bootstrap distribution is clearly skewed to the right. Of special interest here
is that there is strong reason to believe that the actual $F(X)$ looks much
like this bootstrap estimate in this case. Recall that in Figure 1.4, the
Monte Carlo estimate of the $F(X)$ has quite the same shape as the
bootstrap estimate in Figure 3.2. Further, the truncation of the left side
of the bootstrap sampling distribution reduces the chances of (in the
normal approximation case) or prevents (in the percentile-$t$, percentile,
and BC cases) the development of confidence intervals containing
values for $\overline{X}$ that do not occur in the data. For example, although it is
logically impossible for a state to produce a negative number of barrels
of oil in a year, the parametric confidence interval (not shown) around
this mean contains negative numbers and the bootstrap confidence
intervals do not. Any truncated variable could exhibit this sort of
problem, and the bootstrap could be used to resolve it.

Many variables of concern to social scientists are distributed asymmetrically, such as in the experiment above, including any truncated

variable, such as income, education, or any per capita measure. There-fore, the bootstrap might be appropriate for small sample means of these variables. A less familiar type of nonnormality involves multimodality. If a variable has two or more peaks in its distribution, we cannot assume its mean will be normally distributed in small samples, and that the parametric standard deviation formula will accurately estimate the true standard deviation.

A very commonly used variable with such a distribution is the ratings of members of Congress done by the Americans for Democratic Action (ADA). These ratings, based on the representatives' votes on a few key bills, are used widely by political scientists to measure the individuals' conservatism/liberalism (e.g., Dougan & Munger, 1989; Johannes & McAdams, 1981; Kritzer, 1978). Because of the nature of its construc-tion (and perhaps the nature of the underlying variable), the distribution of ADA scores is bimodal, with a peak at each end of the 0-100 scale.[19] Indeed, perhaps all such interest groups' ratings of members of Con-gress have this sort of distribution (Snyder, 1992).

Table 3.2 displays the results of a Monte Carlo experiment testing confidence intervals around the mean of a bimodally distributed vari-able. These data indicate that the bimodality of this variable tends to cause an upward bias in estimates of the dispersion of the sampling distribution, resulting in confidence intervals that are uniformly too wide, compared with the Monte Carlo estimate. The Monte Carlo estimate of the sampling distribution is normal (not shown), but it is narrower than either the bootstrap or the parametric estimate. This is caused by the relatively short, thick tails and central trough of the bimodal distribution. As a result, these overly wide intervals all under-shoot the nominal $\alpha$ level. However, all the bootstrap intervals (except for the percentile-$t$) are narrower and reflect the nominal $\alpha$ level better than does the parametric interval, with no loss of efficiency in the endpoint estimates. The fact that the normal approximation approach comes closest to the Monte Carlo estimates likely reflects the fact that the sampling distribution of this mean is symmetric and probably normal, based on a K-S test.

In Table 3.3, we report the results of developing confidence intervals around the mean ADA score of a sample of 30 members of the U.S. House of Representatives, 99th Congress. As noted, ADA scores are bimodally distributed, as well as truncated at 0 and 100. The relative performance of the confidence interval approaches is the same here as in Table 3.2. The bootstrap intervals are generally narrower than the

TABLE 3.2

The Mean of a Bimodal Variable—Monte Carlo Experiment Results

| | $\alpha/2$ Endpoint | $1 - \alpha/2$ Endpoint | $\alpha$ Level[a] |
|---|---|---|---|
| Monte Carlo estimate | −0.370 | 0.435 | — |
| Parametric[b] | −0.433 (.206)[c] | 0.473 (.206) | .030 |
| Normal approximation[b] | −0.401 (.205) | 0.441 (.205) | .043 |
| Percentile | −0.406 (.207) | 0.447 (.206) | .039 |
| BC | −0.388 (.206) | 0.454 (.207) | .041 |
| Percentile-$t$ | −0.436 (.208) | 0.478 (.208) | .031 |

NOTE: Nominal $\alpha$ level = .05; $B$ = 1,000; $n$ = 25. Monte Carlo $\overline{X}$ = 0.020 (s.d. = .196); bootstrap $\overline{X}^*$ = 0.020 (s.d. = .215).
a. Proportion of the trials that the true value of $\mu$ was left out of the confidence interval. The true value of $\mu$ equals 0, as defined by the random number generator.
b. Using $t_{.025;df=24}$ = 2.064 for both the parametric and normal approximation intervals.
c. Standard deviation of the confidence interval endpoint estimate.

parametric. Given that the Monte Carlo experiment indicated that the true interval is narrow, it is likely that the bootstrap is outperforming the parametric approach here.

The results of these and other analyses in this chapter are largely illustrative. No thorough empirical evaluation has been conducted here or elsewhere, and the exact circumstances under which this differential performance occurs have not been fully documented in the literature. This is especially true with our real-data examples, because we have no

TABLE 3.3

Confidence Intervals Around the Mean ADA Score of a Sample of 30 Members of the U.S. House of Representatives, 99th Congress

| | $\alpha/2$ Endpoint | $\overline{X}$ (s.d) | $1 - \alpha/2$ Endpoint |
|---|---|---|---|
| Parametric ($t$ test) | 30.44 | 44.37 (6.80)[a] | 58.19 |
| Normal approximation | 30.66 | | 58.09 |
| Percentile | 31.23 | 44.37 (6.72) | 58.02 |
| BC | 30.12 | | 58.2 |
| Percentile-$t$ | 30.75 | | 58.38 |

SOURCE: Data from Krehbiel (1990).
NOTE: Nominal $\alpha$ level = .05; $B$ = 1,000.
a. Standard deviation of the estimate.

knowledge of the true sampling distributions in these cases, so we cannot make firm judgments about which interval is most accurate. Many factors will influence this performance, some of which we know in a real-data situation (e.g., the statistic being used, any logical truncation of the variable), but many of which we do not know (e.g., any population characteristic). When one is faced with conflicting inferences from different techniques, two tacks should likely be taken. First, using the information available, determine which approach seems most justifiable a priori. For example, if confidence intervals around a statistic include values that are logically impossible (e.g., a mean age of −16), a researcher should reject the conclusions of that interval. The second approach to dealing with conflicting results would be to report all results and allow the reader to make an independent judgment.

Setting aside these problems with evaluating real-data situations, the various experiments reported in this monograph raise three important points. First, these interval techniques perform differently from one another. And, as will be seen below, no interval performs consistently best on almost any criteria across different circumstances. Second, there is no absolute "best" confidence interval approach to use under all circumstances. Different criteria provide different "winners" for even the same empirical circumstance. For example, in Table 3.1, although the percentile-$t$ has the best overall error rate, the normal approximation yields the least biased estimate of the $\alpha/2$ endpoint. But the final, and perhaps most important, point that these analyses raise is that under a variety of plausible situations, the parametric approach is biased in its estimation of both the confidence interval endpoints and the nominal $\alpha$ level of these intervals. We find that there are indeed situations in which one or more of the bootstrap approaches outperforms the parametric approach.

## The Difference Between Two Sample Medians

Although under certain conditions the sample mean has a known sampling distribution and analytic formulas for estimating the parameters of this distribution, this is not the case for all statistics of interest to social scientists. One such statistic is the difference between two sample medians. There is no theoretical reason to believe this statistic is normally distributed, and even if we wanted to make this assumption, there exists no analytic formula for estimating its standard error. In order to make inferences about the difference between two medians in a population using the parametric approach, one might resort to an indicator about which we know more: the difference between two sample means. But this would be a less-than-ideal indicator if the medians were of interest, and if the distribution of at least one of the underlying variables was asymmetric.

In certain situations, the median takes on a special theoretical importance. In voting under majority rule, for example, it is the median voter preference that determines an election's outcome. In cases where the median preferences of one group (e.g., a congressional committee) are compared with those of another group (e.g., the entire chamber), the researcher using traditional inferential statistics has two choices. First, an inappropriate statistic for which the parametric approach works may be applied (e.g., the difference between two sample means), thereby risking bias in that a less-than-ideal indicator is used (e.g., Canon, 1987, p. 477; Hall & Grofman, 1990, p. 1155; Krehbiel, 1990, p. 144). Alternatively, the researcher may fail to use any statistical test at all, and simply rely on the point estimate (e.g., Sinclair, 1989, pp. 108-111). Either approach is less than ideal.

Bootstrapping allows the testing of the appropriate statistic for the question and data at hand. A straightforward application of the bootstrapping principle in the case of the difference between two sample medians is as follows. First, we draw a sample from the population to which we would like to infer. Second, we calculate the difference between the medians of a characteristic of the two groups based on the original sample. This is our point estimate of the population difference between these medians. Third, we draw $B$ resamples of size $n$ from the original sample. In each resample, we calculate the median value of these groups and take the difference between these medians. The distribution developed by giving a probability of $1/B$ to each value of these bootstrapped differences between the resample medians is the bootstrap estimate of the sampling distribution of this statistic.

Table 3.4 displays the results of a Monte Carlo experiment developing confidence intervals around a difference between the medians of two log-normally distributed variables, where $n_1 = 25$, $n_2 = 25$, and $\theta = 0$. Because there is no parametric method for developing confidence intervals for this parameter, we conduct this Monte Carlo experiment only on the bootstrap intervals.

The pattern of error in Table 3.4 is reminiscent of that of the sampling distribution of the bimodal small sample mean (Table 3.2). This is not surprising, because both of these estimated sampling distributions are

TABLE 3.4

Difference Between the Medians of Two Log-Normal
Variables—Monte Carlo Experiment Results

| | $\alpha/2$ Endpoint | $1 - \alpha/2$ Endpoint | $\alpha$ Level[a] |
|---|---|---|---|
| Monte Carlo estimate | −0.747 | 0.700 | — |
| Normal approximation[b] | −0.830 (.432)[c] | 0.807 (.400) | .025 |
| Percentile | −0.840 (.484) | 0.810 (.454) | .030 |
| BC | −0.695 (.461) | 0.938 (.502) | .043 |
| Percentile-$t$ | −0.924 (.536) | 0.890 (.495) | .026 |

NOTE: Nominal $\alpha$ level = .05; $B$ = 1,000; $n$ = 25. Monte Carlo estimate of difference in medians = −0.006 (s.d. = .361); bootstrap estimate of difference in medians = −0.011 (s.d. = .418).
a. Proportion of the trials that the true value of the difference in medians was left out of the confidence interval. The true difference of medians equals 0, as defined by the random number generator.
b. $\hat{\sigma}_{\hat{\theta}}^{*}$ = 0.416; $t_{.025;df=24}$ = 2.064.
c. Standard deviation of the confidence interval endpoint estimate.

skewed. All of the intervals are too wide, yielding $\alpha$ levels that are lower than the nominal. Each bootstrap interval (save the BC) also reflects the asymmetry of the Monte Carlo interval around the true $\theta$ and the skew of the sampling distribution. The BC method shifts the interval to the right against this asymmetry, resulting in an asymmetry in the opposite direction. This shifting in the BC results in what is the most accurate interval overall, with a .043 $\alpha$ level. Regardless of the performance of these bootstrap intervals, however, it must be emphasized that because this is a case where no parametric alternative exists, the fact that the bootstrap provides *any* method for making inferences is an important contribution.

As an empirical example of the usefulness of the bootstrap in such a situation, consider the issue of the difference between the median preferences of a legislative committee and the entire chamber, as mentioned above. If this difference is nonzero, it means that there is a bias in the committee's preference compared with the chamber's. And if the committee has greater influence on legislative output than the mere votes of its members would afford it (e.g., if committee decisions are routinely deferred to by the chamber), the laws produced by that body might also be biased in terms of not reflecting the majority opinion of the chamber.

Table 3.5 compares the bootstrap confidence intervals around this type of a committee-chamber preference median difference in the U.S.

TABLE 3.5

Hypothesis Tests on the Difference Between Median ADA Scores
of the Committees and Full Chamber in U.S. House of
Representatives, 99th Congress

| Committee | Parametric Difference of Means Test[a] (Krehbiel, 1990) | Bootstrap Difference of Medians Test[b] | | | |
| | | Normal Approximation | Percentile | BC | Percentile-t |
|---|---|---|---|---|---|
| Aging | | | | | |
| Agriculture | | | | | |
| Appropriations | | | | | |
| Armed Services | * | * | * | * | * |
| Banking and Finance | | | | | |
| Budget | | | | | |
| Commerce | | | | | |
| DC | * | | | | |
| Education and Labor | * | | | | |
| Foreign Affairs | * | | * | * | * |
| Government Operations | | | | | |
| Administration | | | | | |
| Interior | | | | | |
| Judiciary | | | | | |
| Merchant Marine and Fisheries | | | | | |
| Post Office | * | * | | | |
| Public Works | | | | | |
| Rules | | | | | |
| Science and Technology | | | | | |
| Small Business | | | | | |
| Standards of Official Conduct | | | | | |
| Veterans' Affairs | | | | | |
| Ways and Means | | | | | |

SOURCE: Data from Krehbiel (1990).
NOTE: Nominal $\alpha = .05$; $B = 1,000$.
a. Significant result of a parametric difference of means $t$ test.
b. Bootstrapped confidence intervals around the difference of medians that do not contain zero.

54

House of Representatives in the 99th Congress. Krehbiel (1990, p. 154) suggests that the differences between the median ADA scores (see above) for committees and the full chamber would be useful in testing the common wisdom that committees are preference outliers. But he resorts to using a difference of *means* test because of the problem discussed above.

Bootstrapping offers a more theoretically pleasing alternative. The bootstrap confidence intervals around the difference between the medians in these data fail to contain zero even fewer times than the difference in means tests against a null of zero. The Armed Services and Foreign Affairs Committees appear to be preference outliers, but there is weaker evidence for the outlier status of the other three committees Krehbiel identifies. This substantiates Krehbiel's hypothesis of unbiasedness more strongly than his analysis does, but, more important, it is more correct theoretically, as the statistic of interest is being tested directly. It should also be noted that had these ADA scores been more asymmetrically distributed,[20] the discrepancy between the medians and means tests would likely have been even greater.

## Inference When Traditional
## Distributional Assumptions Are Violated

As has been discussed at length, parametric inference requires the assumption that the statistic of interest has some known, standard sampling distribution. Confidence intervals and hypothesis tests may then be developed using tabled probability points from this standard distribution. The accuracy of probability statements developed from these confidence intervals therefore rests on the validity of this parametric assumption (see the section on traditional parametric statistical inference in Chapter 1). Distributional assumptions of this sort are often violated, however; even the relatively weak assumption of symmetricality is often invalid (Efron, 1981b, p. 151). And if the distributional assumption is violated, inferential errors could be made at a greater than nominal rate.

The bootstrap has sometimes been used as a check on model assumption violations, in conjunction with parametric inference. Typically, an analyst will report the bootstrapped standard error of a statistic in a footnote, and indicate how close it is to the standard error that was derived analytically (e.g., Green & Krasno, 1990; King, 1991; Poole &

Rosenthal, 1991). This is done to assure the reader that possible assumption violations have not adversely affected the parametric inferences. Although this approach has the disadvantages of the normal approximation confidence interval method (i.e., failing to take advantage of the entire $\hat{F}^*[\hat{\theta}^*]$ and assuming normality for $F[\hat{\theta}]$), it is an entirely legitimate use of the bootstrap.

Other researchers have used the bootstrap in cases of violation of traditional parametric assumptions by abandoning parametric inference altogether. Recent examples of this in the social sciences include bootstrapping a correlation coefficient in the face of nonbivariate normality (Goodall, 1990); bootstrapping marginal costs, output and cost elasticities, and Allen elasticities of substitution under nonnormality (Eakin, McMillen, & Buono, 1990); and bootstrapping logit coefficients from small samples (Teebagy & Chatterjee, 1989).

Strictly speaking, the violation of a parametric assumption is merely a special case of having a statistic without a known sampling distribution. For example, if we would use a traditional $t$ test on the small sample mean of a bimodal variable, we would be violating the tacit assumption of normality. This would have the detrimental effect on our confidence intervals outlined above. In this monograph, we separate the cases of unknown sampling distributions and model assumption violations to suggest different angles on the problem.

## OLS Regression With a Nonnormal Error Structure

In the social sciences, one of the statistical procedures that is most commonly understood to be affected by distributional assumptions is the OLS estimation of regression parameters. In order to make inferential statements using OLS, we need to assume that the random error in the model is normally distributed (Draper & Smith, 1981, p. 23). This assumption is required because the sampling distribution of the OLS estimator is based on the random error of the model. If this parametric assumption holds, we can accurately develop confidence intervals for these coefficients using the $z$ or $t$ table. If we assume normality when the error is in fact not normal, our confidence intervals and hypothesis tests could have a greater than nominal probability of error. Bootstrapping may be a way of overcoming this problem (Freedman, 1984; Freedman & Peters, 1984; Shorack, 1982).

One situation where the error in a regression model could be nonnormal is when the dependent variable is highly skewed. Because the independent variables in an OLS regression model are assumed to be fixed, the distribution of the error structure is entirely determined by the dependent variable. Therefore, if the dependent variable is highly skewed, the assumption of a normal error structure is likely to be violated, at least in small samples. This skew could be the result of the dependent variable being bounded by zero and/or having a few cases with extreme values. Many aggregated variables fit this description (e.g., per capita income, average educational level, literacy rates), and this is a common situation in cross-national and cross-state analysis.

This skew could also be the result of the dependent variable being the mixture of two distributions with different means, especially where one of the distributions has only a few cases in the sample (Everitt & Hand, 1981). This may well appear as an outlier in the data set if the sample size is small (Beckman & Cook, 1983). For example, the level of a certain pollutant may be distributed in a given manner in a river, but a highly polluted tributary may have a different distribution of it. Downstream from the tributary (but not far enough down for the stream's pollutant to become thoroughly mixed with the river's), the levels of random samples of the pollutant will exhibit a mixed distribution. Failure to recognize this mixture would lead to a measured pollutant variable with a skewed distribution.

In Table 3.6, we display the results of a Monte Carlo experiment where a uniform variable with a gamma distributed (shape parameter = 3) error component was regressed on a single continuous independent variable.[21] Because the independent variable values are fixed in this experiment, we use the residuals resampling approach. Our findings indicate that the percentile-$t$ again reflects the nominal $\alpha$ level most accurately. The other intervals (including the parametric) are too narrow, yielding $\alpha$ levels that are too high. The BC method again appears to overcompensate for the skew in the sampling distribution, reducing the bias in the upper endpoint and increasing it in the lower endpoint. Further, note that the standard errors of the interval endpoints are all comparable, but are uniformly larger for the upper endpoint. This is as we would expect in the thin tail of a skewed distribution where more variation is possible. It is also important to note that the sample size of 25 here is close to what statistics texts advise students the central limit theorem allows for the assumption of normality regardless of the shape of the error distribution. This indicates that at least for the percentile-$t$ under these conditions, the asymptotics of the bootstrap appear to come into play more quickly than those of the central limit theorem.

TABLE 3.6
OLS Regression Coefficient With Skewed Error—
Monte Carlo Experiment Results

| | $\alpha/2$ Endpoint | $1 - \alpha/2$ Endpoint | $\alpha$ Level[a] |
|---|---|---|---|
| Monte Carlo estimate | .397 | 3.530 | — |
| Parametric[b] | .489 (.834)[c] | 3.558 (.877) | .063 |
| Normal approximation[b] | .549 (.833) | 3.496 (.871) | .076 |
| Percentile | .524 (.839) | 3.519 (.877) | .072 |
| BC | .586 (.836) | 3.539 (.881) | .077 |
| Percentile-$t$ | .379 (.836) | 3.663 (.888) | .051 |

NOTE: Nominal $\alpha$ level = .05; $B$ = 1,000; $n$ = 25; $r^2$ = .20. Monte Carlo $\hat{B}$ = 2.024 (s.d. = .743); E($\hat{B}^*$) = 2.023 (s.d. = .752). Residuals resampling. Error distribution: $\epsilon \sim \Gamma(3.0)$.
a. Proportion of the trials that the true value of $B_1$ (2.0, as defined by the random number generator) was left out of the confidence interval.
b. Using $t_{.025;df=24}$ = 2.064 for both the parametric and normal approximation intervals.
c. Standard deviation of the confidence interval endpoint estimate.

Table 3.7 presents the confidence intervals developed around the slope for 1985 education spending per capita in the 50 U.S. states as one of five regressors in a model explaining growth in gross state product as the dependent variable (Dye & Taintor, 1991). The other regressors in this straightforward model are growth in population, unemployment, highway expenditures, and oil production. When estimated using OLS, the residuals of this model were not normally distrib-

TABLE 3.7
Confidence Intervals Around the OLS Slope for 1985 Education
Spending per Capita in U.S. States

| | $\alpha/2$ Endpoint | $\bar{X}$ (s.d) | $1 - \alpha/2$ Endpoint |
|---|---|---|---|
| Parametric ($t$ test) | −5.39 | −3.10 (1.17)[a] | −.81 |
| Normal approximation | −6.26 | | .06 |
| Percentile | −5.92 | −2.61 (1.61) | .87 |
| BC | −8.61 | | −.53 |
| Percentile-$t$ | −5.62 | | .76 |

SOURCE: Data from Dye and Taintor (1991).
NOTE: Nominal $\alpha$ level = .05; $B$ = 1,000; $n$ = 50. Cases resampling.
a. Standard deviation of the estimate.

58

uted, as is often the case with cross-state or cross-national aggregated data, owing to a few extreme values in each variable. Further, the OLS estimate for the effect of education spending is negative and statistically significant at the .05 $\alpha$ level, contrary to theoretical expectations. This may be caused by the great influence of Alaska and Wyoming on this model, because of their high levels of per capita spending on education and disastrous lack of economic growth in 1985 caused by a drop in the price of oil.

Three of the bootstrap confidence intervals do contain zero, allowing us to reject the counterintuitive hypothesis, $\hat{\theta} < 0$. However, note that this analysis indicates that the OLS estimate of this coefficient is biased upward, as the bootstrap estimate of the slope is greater than the OLS estimate (see the section on bias estimation in Chapter 2). This bias is of such a magnitude in comparison with the standard error of the OLS estimate that care would need to be taken by the analyst in making inferences. It may be that the BC method is the most accurate in this case, as it is designed to handle bias in $\hat{F}^{*}(\hat{\theta}^{*})$, in which case the parametric inference may well be correct.

# 4. CONCLUSION

This monograph has discussed the basic theory and practice of bootstrapping. The social scientist may find further guidance for the application of and approaches to the bootstrap by examining one of the review articles on the subject that have appeared in the past several years (see, e.g., Diaconis & Efron, 1983; DiCiccio & Efron, 1991; Efron & Tibshirani, 1986; Stine, 1990). In this chapter, we look beyond simple applications to the anticipated developments in the field and the known limitations of the approach.

## Future Work

As a relatively new statistical development that has fascinated many statisticians, theoretical work on the bootstrap has been proceeding at a rapid pace. This research is being pursued in a variety of directions, but there appear to be three particular areas that could be of practical interest to social scientists. First, there is a great amount of activity in applying the technique to an ever-expanding variety of statistics (e.g.,

Basawa, Mallik, McCormick, & Taylor, 1989; Csorgo & Mason, 1989). Some of this work is of a highly specialized nature, such as Leger and Romano's (1990) work on using the bootstrap to pick a trimming proportion for a trimmed mean. But other work here may have broader social scientific applications, such as Sauermann's (1989) work on high-dimensional, sparse log-linear models and Thombs and Schucany's (1990) work on prediction intervals for autoregressive processes.

The second area of continuing research that may hold interest for social scientists is the attempt to reduce the number of bootstrap resamples that are needed to generate a good estimate of the sampling distribution of $\hat{\theta}$ (e.g., Davison, Hinckley, & Schechtman, 1986; Efron, 1990; Hall, 1986; Hinckley, 1988). This typically involves balancing and blocking the resamples to increase their efficiency in representing the sampling distribution of $\hat{\theta}$, in ways analogous to the use of stratified sampling to increase the efficiency of a sample's representation of a population. This work is currently in a very early stage. Whether it will be of any practical use to social scientists remains to be seen, but it seems unlikely. The initial trade-off of computational intensity for distributional assumptions that is made when adopting the bootstrap is based on the presumption of more or less unlimited computing resources. The presumption is largely valid, at least for the range of statistical needs of most social scientists. However, if one were to bootstrap an enormous multiple equation model (e.g., Bianchi et al., 1987) or very complex nonlinear functions, some of these techniques to increase efficiency might be useful.

The final area of ongoing research into the bootstrap that will interest many social scientists involves the issue of complex sampling. Any sample that restricts selection beyond simple random sampling with replacement is complex and requires special analytic consideration regardless of the inferential approach used (Lee, Forthofer, & Lorimor, 1989, p. 8). Although almost all data used in social scientific analyses come from samples of this nature, this issue is typically ignored. Ignoring complex sampling is justifiable in many cases (Smith, 1983), but its effects on inference can sometimes be important.

Most of the theoretical development of the bootstrap has been carried out under the assumption of simple random sampling in order to reduce mathematical complexity, but some recent work has been done to increase the generalizability of the bootstrap with respect to the original sampling plan. For example, Bickel and Krieger (1989) have worked on developing confidence bands around distributions under conditions of stratified sampling and sampling without replacement. The most ambitious work in this regard, however, has been Rao and Wu's (1988) attempt to generalize the bootstrap to multistage cluster sampling plans. A key problem with these approaches is that the necessary calculations are extremely complex, and it is as yet unclear if the practical benefits in terms of increased accuracy are worth the effort.

## Limitations of the Bootstrap

The discussion and evaluation of the bootstrap in this monograph should make it clear that this technique is not a panacea for all statistical problems. Because the theoretical work on the bootstrap is relatively recent, the limits of its applicability are not entirely understood. It is known, for example, that the bootstrap may fail for statistics that depend on "a very narrow feature of the original sampling process" (Stine, 1990, p. 286) that the resampling process cannot reproduce, for example, the sample maximum (Bickel & Freedman, 1981).

The Monte Carlo experiments in this monograph also provide some hints as to where the bootstrap may and may not be useful. First, it is clear that the bootstrap is a tool for developing *inferential* statistics (i.e., confidence intervals and bias estimators), not point estimators of parameters. The bootstrap point estimator appears to reflect rather than alleviate the bias of the statistics involved (see Chapter 2). The possibility exists of adjusting the bootstrapped sampling distribution to compensate for this bias (in a way analogous to the BC method), but little work has been done in this area. There is also the hint that the percentile-$t$ method may yield more accurate confidence intervals than the other bootstrap methods, but this may be an artifact of the particular statistics and assumption violations we have employed as examples. This finding is merely suggestive, as are all of the experimental findings discussed herein. A thorough empirical study of the bootstrap using these Monte Carlo techniques is required if we are to understand fully the conditions under which this approach is superior to the parametric. One set of situations in which we know the bootstrap is indicated, however, is when no parametric approach exists (e.g., the difference between two medians).

To understand the most important limitation of the bootstrap, however, we must return to the original theoretical justification of the procedure (see Chapter 1). In order for the bootstrap to work, we must be prepared to assume that the empirical distribution function represented by the sample is a good estimator of the population distribution function that generated the sample in the first place. That is, we must believe that a representative sample of all the possible distinct values of the population is found in our data (Rubin, 1981). Two practical situations can threaten this assumption's validity. First, the smaller the sample, the less likely it is that all of the relevant characteristics of the population will be represented (Schenker, 1985). This may be especially problematic for developing bootstrapped confidence intervals, because they rely heavily on the tails of the estimated sampling distribution and it is for these extreme values that any approximation technique is weakest (Nash, 1981). However, in each of the experiments we reported, at least one of the bootstrap confidence intervals outperformed the parametric interval on the crucial criterion of approximating the nominal error rate, even though small samples were used. This suggests that the asymptotics on which the accuracy of the bootstrap relies come into play sooner than those of the central limit theorem for the sample mean and OLS regression coefficients in the instances examined here. The fact that the bootstrap has performed so well in comparison with parametric inference, in even these situations where the latter is commonly held to be quite robust, is perhaps good justification for its application in other circumstances where parametric inference is not so advisable.

The second instance in which we might be less than confident that the EDF accurately reflects the PDF is when the original data are not collected using simple random sampling. As noted above, there is currently work being done on the problem of bootstrapping data from a complex random sample. But the central issue remains as to whether the EDF can be held to be a good estimator of the PDF. It is possible that one could assume this to be the case even with data drawn from a nonprobability sample. The justification of this assumption could perhaps be based on some prior information the researcher has about the sample. Of course, this begins to raise the issue prominent in the development of nonparametric inference in the first place—the desire to minimize a priori data assumptions. The situation may arise, however, in which one would be comfortable assuming that the EDF approximates the PDF, but in which one would be uncomfortable assuming that the statistic of interest has some standard sampling distribution.

In the final analysis, bootstrapping, like all statistical procedures, is no better than the assumptions behind it. That these assumptions are less restrictive than those of traditional parametric inference makes the bootstrap more general, but one must not neglect the fact that they are assumptions nonetheless. As with any statistical technique, no amount of mathematical manipulation or computing power can replace sound substantive reasoning and careful modeling.

## Concluding Remarks

In this monograph we have described what the bootstrap is, how to do it, and why it works. Further, we have provided a few examples of statistical situations where it might be useful to the social scientist. It is clear that the extra effort needed to bootstrap a statistic necessitates that it produce a great deal of benefit to make the procedure worthwhile. This is especially true in that few software programs currently provide procedures for general-purpose bootstrapping (but see the Appendix for some ideas and examples about how to bootstrap using statistical software packages).

The examples we have presented in this monograph show, however, that there are situations where the traditional parametric approach fails, and where the bootstrap could fruitfully augment it. Further, as social scientists realize the statistical freedom bootstrapping offers, more creative and valid statistical modeling could result, especially through the use of uniquely developed maximum likelihood functions.

# APPENDIX: BOOTSTRAPPING
# WITH STATISTICAL SOFTWARE PACKAGES

Because the Monte Carlo simulations presented in this monograph required extensive computational capability, most of the analysis was performed with FORTRAN-based routines that we developed ourselves. For instance, the simulation concerning the difference between two medians (Table 3.4) required more than 10 hours of CPU time on an IBM 3090 supercomputer, even with vector processing. However, bootstrapping actual data can be done on modern microcomputers.

The principal algorithm for bootstrapping involves placing the desired statistical procedure within a loop. The steps are straightforward:

1. Generate a resample with replacement from the original data.
2. Estimate the statistics(s), saving the estimate.

3. Repeat 1 and 2 *B* times.
4. Calculate the confidence intervals from the vector of bootstrapped coefficients. (The percentile and percentile-*t* estimates will require the use of a sort routine.)

This may be done in a straightforward manner in a low-level language such as FORTRAN, BASIC, or GAUSS, but even the high-level languages of statistical software packages can sometimes be manipulated to yield a general bootstrap procedure. For example, SAS can be used to bootstrap by using the DO loop to generate a vector of $\hat{\theta}^{*}$'s and the PROC IML call to manipulate the vector of these bootstrapped estimates (Jacoby, 1992).

RATS is an especially convenient high-level program that can be used for bootstrapping because it has a built-in resampling procedure (BOOT) (Doan, 1992, sec. 10.2). The following is an unannotated version of a RATS program that was used to bootstrap a simple regression model with 141 cases, the results of which are displayed in Figure 1.8:

```
ALL 141
open data C:\WP51\boot\smsa.wk1
DATA(UNIT=data,org=obs,format=wks) 1 141 SMSA Pop $
      HighSc Civlab TPI Crime
compute nB = 1000
declare vector bb(nB)
declare vector sd(nB)
set Incpc = TPI/Pop
linreg Incpc 1 141 resids olscoef
# constant HighSc
compute ob=olscoef(2)
compute seb = sqrt(%seesq*%xx(2,2))
compute pmlci = ob - 1.96*seb
compute pmuci = ob + 1.96*seb
statistics resids 1 141
*                                       Bootstrap Loop
do i=1,nB
          boot b / 1 141
          set dep = Incpc(b(t))
          set x1 = HighSc(b(t))
          linreg(noprint) dep 1 141 resids coef
          # constant x1
          compute bb(i) = coef(2)
          compute sd(i) = sqrt(%seesq*%xx(2,2))
          Display(unit = screen) 'Trial ' i
end do i
```

```
*                           Calculate Confidence Intervals
set c 1 nB = bb(t)
set csd 1 nB = sd(t)
statistics c 1 nB
compute nauci = ob + 1.96*sqrt(%variance)
compute nalci = ob - 1.96*sqrt(%variance)
order c 1 nB csd
print 1 nB c csd
compute il = fix((nB*.05)/2)
compute iu = nB - il + 1
set tscore 1 nB = (bb(t) - ob)/csd(t)
order tscore 1 nB csd
compute ptlci = tscore(il)*seb + ob
compute ptuci = tscore(iu)*seb + ob
set prt 1 nB = %if(c(t) < ob,1,0)
stats(noprint) prt
compute prop = %mean
declare real zp
compute zit = -1.0
until zp > prop {
        compute zp = %cdf(zit)
        compute zit = zit + .001
        }
end until
compute zit = zit - .001
compute ubc = fix(%cdf(2*zit+1.96)*nB)
compute lbc = fix(%cdf(2*zit-1.96)*nB)
if lbc < 1 {
        compute lbc = 1
        }
end if
display '                            lower ci      upper ci
length'
display 'Parametric       ' pmlci pmuci pmuci-pmlci
display 'normal approx ' nalci nauci nauci-nalci
display 'percentile      ' c(il) c(iu) c(iu)-c(il)
display 'percentile t    ' ptlci ptuci ptuci-ptlci
display 'bias-corrected' c(lbc) c(ubc) c(ubc)-c(lbc)
end
```

This program required only 25 minutes to execute on a 386 microcomputer with a 16MHz processor. (An annotated version of this RATS program is available from the authors upon request.) RATS took five minutes to do the analysis done for Figure 3.2, 14 minutes for Table 3.3, and 26 minutes for Table 3.7. Sample size seems to increase the running time more rapidly than does model complication, but iterative estimation approaches (e.g., maximum likelihood) will increase computation time by a factor of the number of iterations conducted.

Some packages have specific bootstrapping options for certain statistics. For example, SPSS-X allows for the bootstrapping of constrained nonlinear regression (CNLR), a very general model (SPSS, 1988, 689-691), and SHAZAM has an option in its OLS regression procedure that generates the bootstrapped standard errors of the coefficients (White, Wong, Whistler, & Haun, 1990, pp. 93-95). The SHAZAM manual also provides an example of a program for bootstrapping regression, the structure of which can be appropriated to bootstrap any statistic that SHAZAM calculates, reports, and stores (White et al., 1990, pp. 214-215). The most formal development of bootstrap procedures is found in STATA, however, which provides a bootstrap command that can take a defined program segment and perform bootstrap resampling and iterative estimation (Computing Resources Center, 1992, pp. 163-166).

# NOTES

1. The K-S test uses the largest difference between the proportions in the same categories of the cumulative distribution function of two variables to test if they have different distributions. In this case, we test the cumulative distribution function of the variable displayed in Figure 1.4 against that of a normal distribution, and thereby reject the normality of this $\bar{X}$'s distribution at the .05 $\alpha$-level (Blalock, 1972, pp. 262-265).

2. In maximum likelihood estimation, the use of the information matrix is a general method for estimating standard errors (Judge, Griffiths, Hill, Lutkepohl, & Lee, 1985, pp. 177-180; King, 1989, pp. 87-90), but this can become intractable for some complex estimators.

3. Groseclose (1992) uses Monte Carlo simulation to estimate this sampling distribution empirically for the 99th Congress, but no general theoretical solution has been found.

4. Although the bootstrap can be used in conjunction with parametric assumptions (e.g., Efron, 1982, sec. 5.2), the most general and interesting manifestation of the technique is in its nonparametric form.

5. This EDF can be simulated by constructing a simple histogram of $x_i$. Although this step is conceptually important to the bootstrap, in practice one need not actually construct the EDF to bootstrap a $\hat{\theta}$.

6. Again, this can be a simple histogram of the $\hat{\theta}_b^*$ 's.

7. If we have other information about the population distribution function, such as empirical or theoretical evidence about its shape or the value of its parameters, we can incorporate them into our calculations, as is done in Bayesian and parametric inferential statistics. However, we are concerned in this monograph with cases where no such reliable information exists.

8. This is because the sampling distribution of $\bar{X}$ is known to be normal in many cases, and analytic formulas for its standard error and expected value exist and are well known.

9. The irregular appearance of this distribution is largely caused by the histogram displaying it having a limited number of categories, the sample EDF being a discrete rather than continuous function, and the random nature of the bootstrap resampling procedure. There is some discussion in the bootstrapping literature of smoothing the EDF to approximate a continuous function more closely (Silverman & Young, 1987), but the practical benefits of this approach are unproven. This is discussed further later in this chapter.

10. If sampling is done without replacement, when $n = N$, $\hat{F} = F$, by definition. Using replacement sampling adds a degree of random error that will make $\hat{F}$ only a very good approximation of $F$ when $n = N$.

11. Schucany, Gray, and Owen (1971) extend the jackknife to estimate higher-order bias, but little practical use has been made of their technique.

12. For our assessment of bias estimation, however, we use 5,000 trials.

13. Type II errors (failing to reject false null hypotheses) are also of concern in evaluating an inferential technique. Monte Carlo simulation of a model under a variety of conditions may be used to evaluate the Type II error of an inferential test (Duval &

66

Groeneveld, 1987). Elsewhere, we have used this technique to test the Type II error rates of the bootstrap, but following the typical emphasis in the social sciences, we focus on Type I errors in this monograph (Mooney & Duval, 1992).

14. Although the interpretation of the probabilities involving confidence intervals is problematic (King, 1989, pp. 14-17), we follow the traditional notation and interpretation throughout this monograph.

15. See Hall (1988b) for a discussion of seven such methods.

16. The concern has also been raised that $\hat{F}^*(\hat{\theta}^*)$ may have a different degree of skew than $F(\hat{\theta})$ (Schenker, 1985). Efron (1987) has proposed the $BC_a$ method to address this concern. In addition to $z_0$, the $BC_a$ uses an acceleration constant, $a$, based on the skew of $\hat{F}^*(\hat{\theta}^*)$, to adjust the percentile points of $\hat{F}^*(\hat{\theta}^*)$ to be used in a confidence interval. Unlike $z_0$, however, the acceleration constant is often difficult or impossible to calculate from $\hat{F}^*(\hat{\theta}^*)$ for a given $\hat{\theta}$ (DiCiccio & Romano, 1988; Hall, 1988b). And as the emphasis in this monograph is on the practical use of the bootstrap, we do not further describe or compare the $BC_a$ with the other techniques. For further information on the $BC_a$, see Efron (1987), DiCiccio and Tibshirani (1987), and especially DiCiccio and Efron (1991), who develop a promising practical approach to calculating $a$.

17. The general case of the BC method allows the analyst to specify that these variables, $\hat{\varphi} - \varphi$ and $\hat{\varphi}^* - \hat{\varphi}$, are distributed in any known way (DiCiccio & Romano, 1988). The normal distribution is used because of its familiarity and the availability of a set of tabled values for the adjustment of the bootstrapped sampling distribution.

18. See Rao and Wu (1988) and Bickel and Freedman (1984) on the possibility of using the bootstrap in complex sampling situations.

19. This variable is also truncated at zero and 100, to complicate the situation further.

20. ADA scores tend to be distributed in a symmetrical U-shaped fashion, with more members falling near the extremes of the 0-100 range than the near middle of it.

21. This error is somewhat skewed, but not nearly as skewed as an exponential distribution, for example.

# REFERENCES

AL-SAHLAWI, M. A. (1990) "Forecasting the demand for electricity in Saudi Arabia." Energy Journal 11: 119-125.

ANDERSON, O. D. (1976) Time Series Analysis and Forecasting. Boston: Butterworth.

BABU, G. J., and SINGH, K. (1983) "Inference on means using the bootstrap." Annals of Statistics 11: 999-1003.

BADRINATH, S. G., and CHATTERJEE, S. (1991) "A data-analytic look at skewness and elongation in common-stock-return distributions." Journal of Business and Economic Statistics 9: 223-233.

BARTELS, L. M. (1991) "Instrumental and 'quasi-instrumental' variables." American Journal of Political Science 35: 777-800.

BARTON, A. P. (1962) "Note on unbiased estimation of the squared multiple correlation coefficient." Statistica Neerlandica 16: 151-163.

BASAWA, I. V., MALLIK, A. K., McCORMICK, W. P., and TAYLOR, R. C. (1989) "Bootstrapping explosive autoregressive processes." Annals of Statistics 17: 1479-1486.

BECKMAN, R. J., and COOK, R. D. (1983) "Outliers." Technometrics 25: 119-163.

BIANCHI, C., CALZOLARI, G., and BRILLET, J.-L. (1987) "Measuring forecast uncertainty: A review with evaluation based on a macro model of the French economy." International Journal of Forecasting 3: 211-227.

BICKEL, P. J., and FREEDMAN, D. A. (1981) "Some asymptotics on the bootstrap." Annals of Statistics 9: 1196-1217.

BICKEL, P. J., and FREEDMAN, D. A. (1984) "Asymptotic normality and the bootstrap in stratified sampling." Annals of Statistics 12: 470-481.

BICKEL, P. J., and KRIEGER, A. M. (1989) "Confidence bands for a distribution function using the bootstrap." Journal of the American Statistical Association 84: 95-100.

BLALOCK, H. M., Jr. (1972) Social Statistics (2nd ed.). New York: McGraw-Hill.

BORRELLO, G. M., and THOMPSON, B. (1989) "A replication bootstrap analysis of the structure underlying perceptions of stereotypic love." Journal of General Psychology 116: 317-327.

BRILLINGER, D. R. (1964) "The asymptotic behaviour of Tukey's general method of setting approximate confidence limits (the jackknife) when applied to maximum likelihood estimates." Review of the International Statistical Institute 32: 202-206.

CANON, D. T. (1987) "Actors, athletes, and astronauts: Political amateurs in the United States Congress." Ph.D. dissertation, University of Minnesota.

Computing Resources Center (1992) STATA Reference Manual: Release 3 (Vol. 2, 5th ed.). Santa Monica, CA: Author.

COOK, R. D. (1977) "Detection of influential observations in linear regression." Technometrics 19: 15-18.

CSORGO, S., and MASON, D. M. (1989) "Bootstrapping empirical functions." Annals of Statistics 17: 1447-1471.

69

DAVISON, A. C., HINCKLEY, D. V., and SCHECHTMAN, E. (1986) "Efficient bootstrap simulation." Biometrika 73: 555-566.
DIACONIS, P., and EFRON, B. (1983) "Computer intensive methods in statistics." Scientific American 248: 5, 116-130.
DiCICCIO, T. J., and EFRON, B. (1991) "More accurate confidence intervals in exponential families." Technical report no. 368, Department of Statistics, Stanford University, Stanford, CA.
DiCICCIO, T. J., and ROMANO, J. P. (1988) "A review of bootstrap confidence intervals" (with discussion). Journal of the Royal Statistical Society, Series B, 50: 338-370.
DiCICCIO, T. J., and ROMANO, J. P. (1989) "The automatic percentile method: Accurate confidence limits in parametric models." Canadian Journal of Statistics 17: 155-169.
DiCICCIO, T. J., and TIBSHIRANI, R. (1987) "Bootstrap confidence intervals and bootstrap approximations." Journal of the American Statistical Association 82: 163-170.
DOAN, T. A. (1992) RATS User's Manual: Version 4. Evanston, IL: Estima.
DOUGAN, W. R., and MUNGER, M. C. (1989) "The rationality of ideology." Journal of Law and Economics 32: 119-142.
DOUGLAS, S. M. (1987) "Improving the estimation of a switching regressions model: An analysis of problems and improvements using the bootstrap." Ph.D. dissertation, University of North Carolina, Chapel Hill.
DRAPER, N. R., and SMITH, H. (1981) Applied Regression Analysis (2nd ed.). New York: John Wiley.
DUVAL, R. D., and GROENEVELD, L. (1987) "Hidden policies and hypothesis tests: The implications of Type II errors for environmental regulation." American Journal of Political Science 31: 423-447.
DYE, T. R., and TAINTOR, J. B. (1991) States: The Fiscal Data Book. Tallahassee: Florida State University, Policy Sciences Program.
EAKIN, B. K., McMILLEN, D. P., and BUONO, M. J. (1990) "Constructing confidence intervals using the bootstrap: An application to a multi-product cost function." Review of Economics and Statistics 72: 339-344.
EFRON, B. (1979) "Bootstrap methods: Another look at the jackknife." Annals of Statistics 7: 1-26.
EFRON, B. (1981a) "Censored data and the bootstrap." Journal of the American Statistical Association 76: 312-319.
EFRON, B. (1981b) "Nonparametric standard errors and confidence intervals" (with discussion). Canadian Journal of Statistics 9: 139-172.
EFRON, B. (1982) The Jackknife, the Bootstrap, and Other Resampling Plans. Philadelphia: Society for Industrial and Applied Mathematics.
EFRON, B. (1987) "Better bootstrap confidence intervals" (with discussion). Journal of the American Statistical Association 82: 171-200.
EFRON, B. (1990) "More efficient bootstrap computations." Journal of the American Statistical Association 85: 79-89.
EFRON, B., and GONG, G. (1983) "A leisurely look at the bootstrap, the jackknife and cross-validation." American Statistician 37: 36-48.
EFRON, B., and STEIN, C. (1981) "The jackknife estimate of variance." Annals of Statistics 9: 586-596.
EFRON, B., and TIBSHIRANI, R. (1986) "Bootstrap methods for standard errors, confidence intervals, and other measures of statistical accuracy." Statistical Science 1: 54-77.

70

EVERITT, B. S. (1980) Cluster Analysis (2nd ed.). London: Heineman Educational.
EVERITT, B. S., and HAND, D. J. (1981) Finite Mixture Distributions. London: Chapman & Hall.
FAY, R. E. (1985) "A jackknifed chi-square test for complex samples." Journal of the American Statistical Association 80: 148-157.
FREEDMAN, D. A. (1981) "Bootstrapping regression models." Annals of Statistics 9: 1218-1228.
FREEDMAN, D. A. (1984) "On bootstrapping two-stage least squares estimates in stationary linear models." Annals of Statistics 12: 827-842.
FREEDMAN, D. A., and PETERS, S. C. (1984) "Bootstrapping a regression equation: Some empirical results." Journal of the American Statistical Association 79: 97-106.
GOODALL, C. (1990) "A simple objective method for determining a percent standard in mixed reimbursement systems." Journal of Health Economics 9: 253-271.
GREEN, D. P., and KRASNO, J. S. (1990) "Rebuttal to Jacobson's 'New evidence for old arguments.'" American Journal of Political Science 34: 363-372.
GROSECLOSE, T. (1992) Median-Based Tests of Committee Composition. Pittsburgh, PA: Carnegie Mellon University, Department of Social and Decision Sciences.
HALL, P. (1986) "On the number of bootstrap simulations required to construct a confidence interval." Annals of Statistics 14: 1453-1462.
HALL, P. (1988a) "On symmetric bootstrap confidence intervals." Journal of the Royal Statistical Society, Series B, 50: 35-45.
HALL, P. (1988b) "Theoretical comparison of bootstrap confidence intervals" (with discussion). Annals of Statistics 16: 927-985.
HALL, R. L., and GROFMAN, B. (1990) "The committee assignment process and the conditional nature of committee bias." American Political Science Review 84: 1149-1166.
HANUSHEK, E. A., and JACKSON, J. E. (1977) Statistical Methods for Social Scientists. New York: Academic Press.
HARRIS, D. J., and KOLEN, M. J. (1989) "Examining the stability of Angoff's delta item bias statistic using the bootstrap." Educational and Psychological Measurement 49: 81-87.
HINCKLEY, D. W. (1978) "Improving the jackknife with special reference to correlation estimation." Biometrika 65: 13-22.
HINCKLEY, D. W. (1988) "Bootstrap methods." Journal of the Royal Statistical Society, Series B, 50: 321-337.
JACOBY, W. G. (1992) PROC IML Statements for Creating a Bootstrap Distribution of OLS Regression Coefficients (Assuming Random Regressors). Columbia: University of South Carolina.
JOHANNES, J., and McADAMS, J. (1981) "The congressional incumbency effect: Is it casework, policy compatibility, or something else?" American Journal of Political Science 25: 512-542.
JOLLIFFE, I. T. (1972) "Discarding variables in a principal components model, I: Artificial data." Applied Statistics 21: 160-173.
JONES, H. L. (1956) "Investigating the properties of a sample mean by employing random sub-sample means." Journal of the American Statistical Association 51: 54-83.
JUDGE, G. G., GRIFFITHS, W. E., HILL, R. C., LUTKEPOHL, H., and LEE, T.-C. (1985) The Theory and Practice of Econometrics (2nd ed.). New York: John Wiley.
KING, G. (1989) Unifying Political Methodology: The Likelihood Theory of Statistical Inference. New York: Cambridge University Press.
KING, G. (1991) "Constituency Service and Incumbency Advantage." British Journal of Political Science 21: 119-128.

KREHBIEL, K. (1990) "Are congressional committees composed of preference outliers?" American Political Science Review 84: 149-163.

KRITZER, H. M. (1978) "Ideology and American political elites." Public Opinion Quarterly 42: 484-502.

LAMBERT, Z. V., WILDT, A. R., and DURAND, R. M. (1989) "Approximate confidence intervals for estimates of redundancy between sets of variables." Multivariate Behavioral Research 24: 307-333.

LAMBERT, Z. V., WILDT, A. R., and DURAND, R. M. (1990) "Assessing sampling variation relative to number of factors criteria." Educational and Psychological Measurement 50: 33-48.

LEE, E. S., FORTHOFER, R. N., and LORIMOR, R. J. (1989) Analyzing Complex Survey Data. Sage University Paper series on Quantitative Applications in the Social Sciences, 07-071. Newbury Park, CA: Sage.

LEGER, C., and ROMANO, J. P. (1990) "Bootstrap adaptive estimation: The trimmed-mean example." Canadian Journal of Statistics 18: 297-314.

LIU, R. Y., and SINGH, K. (1988) [Discussion of Hall]. Annals of Statistics 16: 978-979.

LOH, W.-Y., and WU, C. F. J. (1987) [Comment on Efron]. Journal of the American Statistical Association 82: 188-190.

MANSFIELD, E. (1986) Basic Statistics. New York: W. W. Norton.

MANTEL, N. (1967) "Assumption-free estimators using U statistics and a relationship to the jackknife method." Biometrics 23: 567-571.

MARITZ, J. S. (1981) Distribution-Free Statistical Methods. New York: Chapman & Hall.

MASON, R., and BROWN, W. G. (1975) "Multicollinearity problems and ridge regression in sociological models." Social Science Research 4: 135-149.

McCARTHY, P. J. (1969) "Pseudo-replication: Half-samples." Review of the International Statistical Institute 37: 239-264.

MILLER, R. G. (1964) "A trustworthy jackknife." Annals of Mathematical Statistics 35: 1594-1605.

MILLER, R. G. (1974) "The jackknife: A review." Biometrika 61: 1-15.

MOHR, L. B. (1990) Understanding Significance Testing. Sage University Paper series on Quantitative Applications in the Social Sciences, 07-073. Newbury Park, CA: Sage.

MOONEY, C. Z., and DUVAL, R. D. (1992, September) "Bootstrap inference: A preliminary Monte Carlo evaluation." Presented at the annual meeting of the American Political Science Association, Chicago.

NASH, S. W. (1981) [Discussion of Efron]. Canadian Journal of Statistics 9: 163-164.

NOREEN, E. W. (1989) Computer-Intensive Methods for Testing Hypotheses. New York: John Wiley.

POOLE, K. T., and ROSENTHAL, H. (1991) "Patterns of congressional voting." American Journal of Political Science 35: 228-278.

QUENOUILLE, M. H. (1949) "Approximate tests of correlation in time-series." Journal of the Royal Statistical Society, Series B, 11: 68-84.

QUENOUILLE, M. H. (1956) "Notes on bias in estimation." Biometrika 43: 353-360.

RAO, B. L. S. P. (1987) Asymptotic Theory of Statistical Inference. New York: John Wiley.

RAO, J. N. K., and BEEGLE, L. D. (1967) "A Monte Carlo study of some ratio estimators." Sankhya B29: 47-56.

RAO, J. N. K., and WU, C. F. J. (1988) "Resampling inference with complex survey data." Journal of the American Statistical Association 83: 231-241.

ROHATGI, V. K. (1984) Statistical Inference. New York: John Wiley.

RUBIN, D. B. (1981) "The Bayesian bootstrap." Annals of Statistics 9: 130-134.

SAUERMANN, W. (1989) "Bootstrapping the maximum likelihood estimator in high-dimensional log-linear models." Annals of Statistics 17: 1198-1216.

SCHENKER, N. (1985) "Qualms about bootstrap confidence intervals." Journal of the American Statistical Association 80: 360-361.

SCHUCANY, W. R., GRAY, H. L., and OWEN, D. B. (1971) "On bias reduction in estimation." Journal of the American Statistical Association 66: 524-533.

SELVANATHAN, E. A. (1989) "A note on the stochastic approach to index numbers." Journal of Business and Economic Statistics 7: 471-474.

SHAO, J. (1988) "Bootstrap variance and bias estimation in linear models." Canadian Journal of Statistics 16: 371-382.

SHORACK, G. R. (1982) "Bootstrapping robust regression." Communications in Statistics: Theory and Methods 11: 961-972.

SILVERMAN, B., and YOUNG, A. (1987) "The bootstrap: To smooth or not to smooth?" Biometrika 74: 469-479.

SINCLAIR, B. (1989) The Transformation of the U.S. Senate. Baltimore: Johns Hopkins University Press.

SINGH, K. (1981) "On the asymptotic accuracy of Efron's bootstrap." Annals of Statistics 9: 1187-1195.

SINGH, K. (1986) [Discussion of Wu]. Annals of Statistics 14: 1328-1330.

SMITH, T. M. F. (1983) "On the validity of inferences from non-random samples." Journal of the Royal Statistical Society, Series A, 146: 394-403.

SNYDER, J. M., Jr. (1992) "Artificial extremism in interest group ratings." Legislative Studies Quarterly 17: 319-345.

SOBOL, I. M. (1975) The Monte Carlo Method. Moscow: MIR.

SPSS, Inc. (1988) SPSS-X User's Guide (3rd ed.). Chicago: Author.

SRIVASTAVA, M. S., and SINGH, B. (1989) "Bootstrapping in multiplicative models." Journal of Econometrics 42: 287-297.

STINE, R. A. (1985) "Bootstrap prediction intervals for regression." Journal of the American Statistical Association 80: 1026-1031.

STINE, R. A. (1990) "An introduction to bootstrap methods." Sociological Methods and Research 18: 243-291.

TEEBAGY, N., and CHATTERJEE, S. (1989) "Inference in a binary response model with applications to data analysis." Decision Sciences 20: 393-403.

THOMBS, L. A., and SCHUCANY, W. R. (1990) "Bootstrap prediction intervals for autoregression." Journal of the American Statistical Society 85: 486-492.

TIBSHIRANI, R. J. (1988) [Discussion of Hinckley, and DiCiccio and Romano.] Journal of the Royal Statistical Society, Series B, 50: 362-363.

TIKU, M. L., TAN, W. Y., and BALAKRISHNAN, N. (1986) Robust Inference. New York: Marcel Dekker.

TUKEY, J. (1958) "Bias and confidence in not-quite large samples" (abstract). Annals of Mathematical Statistics 29: 614.

U.S. Bureau of the Census (1979) State and Metropolitan Data Book (Statistical Abstract Supplement). Washington, DC: Government Printing Office.

VEALL, M. R. (1987) "Bootstrapping the probability distribution of peak electricity demand." International Economic Review 28: 203-212.

WHITE, K. J., WONG, S. D., WHISTLER, D., and HAUN, S. A. (1990) SHAZAM Econometrics Computer Program: User's Reference Manual (Version 6.2). New York: McGraw-Hill.

## ABOUT THE AUTHORS

*CHRISTOPHER Z. MOONEY* is Assistant Professor of Political Science at West Virginia University and Visiting Lecturer of Government at the University of Essex, United Kingdom. His teaching and research interests include legislative decision making, U.S. state politics, and political methodology. He received his Ph.D. from the University of Wisconsin—Madison in 1990. His work has appeared in the *Western Political Quarterly, Social Science Quarterly, American Politics Quarterly,* and *Legislative Studies Quarterly.*

*ROBERT D. DUVAL* is Associate Professor of Political Science and Graduate Director of the Program in Public Policy at West Virginia University. His teaching and research interests include security policy, environmental policy, quantitative international politics, and statistical methods. His research has appeared in the *British Journal of Political Science,* the *Journal of Conflict Resolution,* and the *American Journal of Political Science.*